BORDER PUBS & INNS

Allanton - The Allanton Inn

BORDER PUBS & INNS

A Walkers Guide

by

Alan Hall

CICERONE PRESS
MILNTHORPE, CUMBRIA

ISBN 1 85284 172 9
A catalogue record for this book is available from the British Library

Dedicated to my Supportive Family

ACKNOWLEDGEMENTS

To Greta, whose opinions I respect, whose proof-reading I need and whose infectious zest for the entire project I appreciate, my sincere thanks. Thank you also every Landlord and Landlady of all 53 establishments I visited, for your enthusiastic, and in some cases hilarious, cooperation. A pride in the pub, a pride in the Borders, and a pride in your customers made my research a pleasure beyond measure.

My appreciation to Roberta Carruthers for her illustrations, and to Hector and Alastair Innes for their expert photographic advice. Also thanks to Ros Brown, Archivist, Borders Regional Library.

Finally many thanks to all the cheerful customers I met in my travels from pub to pub and walk to walk, characters who drained not only their glasses, but also their barrels of local knowledge. Where better to have one's crack than in a Border pub and what better way to end than with a Border toast - "Wha's Like Us - Gae Few".

All photographs and maps are by the author. The illustrations are by Roberta Carruthers and the introductory quotation is taken from *This Unknown Island* by S.P.B.Mais (Bodley Head).

By the same author: The Border Country - a walkers guide

Front Cover: Mountbenger - Gordon Arms Hotel

CONTENTS

FOREWORD

REFLECTIONS ON AND REASONS FOR A WALKER'S GUIDE TO BORDER PUBS

Researching and writing this guide has put a smile on my face and added a new dimension to the task of introducing this land of legend to the lovers of the Great Outdoors. For it is my sincere wish that it not only brings the reader to the Borderland, but also helps visitors understand and appreciate our countryside and our customs; in fact to put a smile on their faces and a twinkle in their eyes. And as a result derive the same measure of pleasure in exploring the pubs and walks of the Borderland as I did in preparing the guide.

Whether it was because of my greying thatch or the desire to help me with my task, I do not know, for I received no less than 38 offers from "research assistants". Regretfully, I declined the helping hand and the thirsty tongue, as I felt it "no'but right" that the work, no matter how hard and demanding, should be mine and mine alone.

It has not, I may say, been an easy ridge to cross or an easy hill to climb; essential research has involved me in the sampling of 424 pints, a mere 53 gallons of ale, and heaven knows how many bar meals. Research into every aspect of the Border pub as it affects the walker has been of paramount importance, for just as I believe in walking every walk, so do I believe in experiencing every pub. Thankfully my digestion and liver are well and my desire and ability to walk remain unimpaired.

Hopefully this volume will broaden the horizons of Border walkers, for in addition to presenting them with "everything they need to know about Border pubs, plus that little bit more", I have included route directions for 80 walks over rolling hills and windswept fells, along dramatic coastlines and by surging burns and tranquil lochs, in this legendary land. My target has been that the guide will be as necessary a piece of equipment for the Border walker as a map, a compass, a survival bag and a first-aid kit. I hope it provides knowledge about the journey and its end, putting the lie to the commonly held view "that it is better to travel than to arrive" by making the end equal to the journey. To quote John Dodds of Selkirk:

And so, wi' freens sae blithe and cheery,
I'm better fettled, no' sae weary,

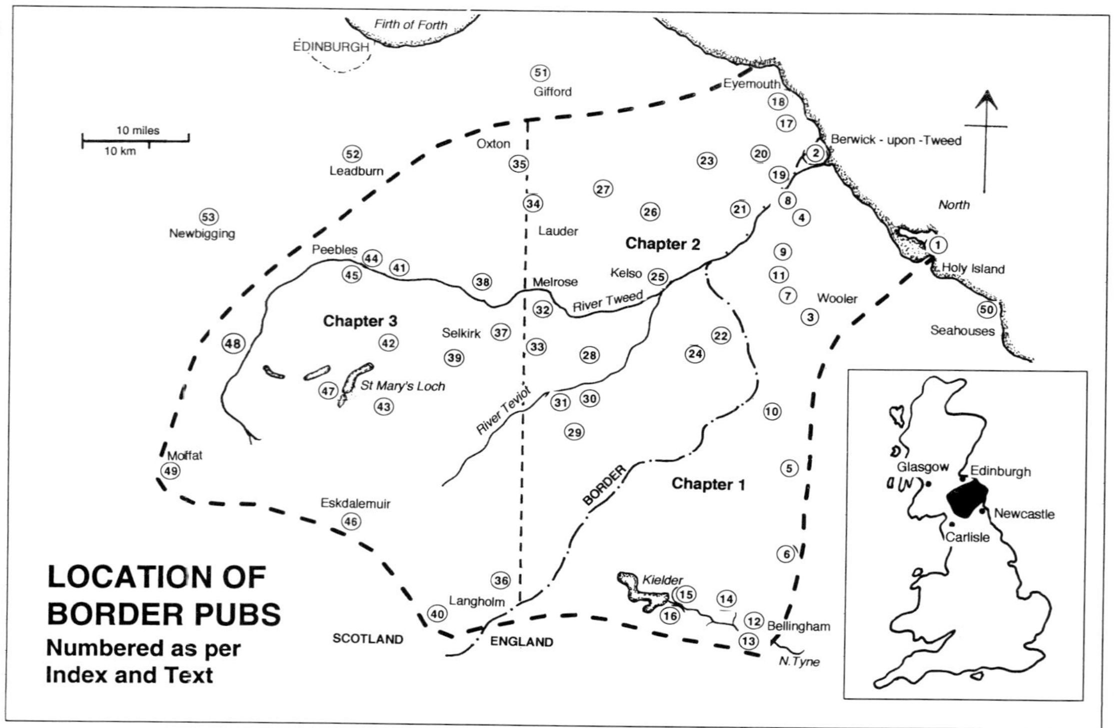
LOCATION OF BORDER PUBS
Numbered as per Index and Text
Chapter 1
Chapter 2
Chapter 3
North
10 miles
10 km
Firth of Forth
EDINBURGH
Gifford
Eyemouth
Berwick - upon -Tweed
Holy Island
Seahouses
Wooler
Oxton
Leadburn
Newbigging
Lauder
Peebles
Melrose
Kelso
River Tweed
Selkirk
St Mary's Loch
River Teviot
BORDER
Moffat
Eskdalemuir
Langholm
SCOTLAND
ENGLAND
Kielder
Bellingham
N.Tyne
Glasgow
Edinburgh
Newcastle
Carlisle

INTRODUCTION

My own inclination is always to make a bee-line for the church and the public house in every village. In the former I get a quick glimpse of its ancient, in the latter a not so quick glimpse of its modern history.

S.P.B.Mais.

I wager these words apply to the vast majority of walkers, be they Sunday strollers or addicted hill-walkers. For when the walking has ended and the reflections begin, what can be finer than corporal and spiritual succour. I would also speculate that at some point in the journey, probably when the adrenalin flow is but a fading trickle, all walkers tend to envisage an inn or pub where the welcome is warm and the beer is cool; a place of like minds and common interests, where all can stretch both legs and thoughts and have their "crack".

Such havens can be difficult to locate, for good walks and good pubs seldom go hand in hand and having found the object of one's desires, chances are it is not "all things to all walkers".

In compiling this small volume I have cast a hungry and thirsty walker's eye over Border Inns, Public Houses, Howffs, Taverns, and Hotels for establishments that are at best "all things to all walkers", or at least, "all things to some walkers" or "some things to all walkers". For we all have, as lovers of the great outdoors, differing ideas and standards of what makes the perfect haven; just as the brewers and landlords have differing ideas regarding the enticement and retention of potential customers. Even the classification of the establishment can be confusing or misleading; in order to obtain a definition, under-stood by all, I consulted the *Twentieth Century Dictionary* of W. & R.Chambers Limited, Edinburgh who define the subject of this work thus:

Public House	a house open to the public, chiefly used for selling beer and other liquors.
Pub	a public house or tavern.
Tavern	a licensed house for the sale of liquors, with accommodation for travellers.
Inn	a public house for the lodging and entertainment of travellers.
Hotel	a superior house for the accommodation of strangers."

It is my considered opinion that inn or pub best define what we are looking for, so let us begin our search for Border Inns and Pubs, even though the odd one may aspire to the suffix Hotel.

A collection of 53 inns/pubs are included. All have one virtue in common: they all provide rest and good cheer for the Border walker.

A walker's pub guide is in its way as necessary to the walker as a map, compass and route guide. For a journey is never complete till succour is sought and the tale is told, or dare I say it, occasionally embellished. Let the parched pedestrian search no longer for comfort and sustenance, for it is the intention of this guide to aid all those in need.

BACKGROUND

History of the Border Pub

Vineyard, Hospice, Rest House, Hostel, Ale House, Howff, Tavern, Coaching Inn, Public House (Pub), Inn and today's "inn" word Hotel have through the ages supplied the weary traveller. The movement of man, aided by the development of the wheel, be it for military, ecclesiastical or commercial reasons, has contributed to the birth of the inn/pub as we know it today.

From the first century invasion of the Romans, to the great medieval movements of armies and clerics, the numbers of Hospices and Rest Houses grew. Then from the fourteenth century the Ale House prospered, rising to a summit in the nineteenth century, when inn-keepers grew fat and the pub reigned supreme. Holy Island, for example, supported at least 10 inns in the mid 1800s, for a population of barely 300.

Farm- or house-brewed ale, originally the main beverage, if of high quality, would attract customers and supplement income, thus spawning the Ale House. With the Union of the Crowns in 1603 came the English licensing laws, when ale-houses were required to be licensed for the sale of beer and spirits. Two Border locals, The Crook Inn at Tweedsmuir and The Spread Eagle in Jedburgh were, along with the Kingshouse of Glen Coe, the first licensed houses in Scotland in 1604.

Local whisky production increased dramatically after the Jacobite campaigns; dissolutioned Highland troops produced their fiery spirit from illicit stills hidden high in Border cleuchs and gullies. French brandy and claret also found its way into Border cellars, be they private houses or country inns, courtesy of the Berwickshire smugglers, with their headquarters around Eyemouth.

Inn names and architecture provide revealing insights into the social history of the region, reflecting the lifestyle, occupations and habits of the population. Fishing communities have The Ship, The Pilot,

The Crown and Anchor; agricultural land The Wheatsheaf and The Black Bull; rivers the Fishers Arms and White Swan; centres of population The Cross Keys (coaching connections) and Fox and Hounds; upland fells and moorland The Blackcock, Hart Manor and The Crook.

ACTION

The area known as The Borders, in truth, recognizes no national boundary, for the walker's needs are as keen on the Northumbrian Cheviots as by Berwickshire's cliffs or astride the Tweedsmuir Hills; and for the purpose of this guide I have imposed a legendary boundary - Hall's Wall, within which resides The Border Pub.

From Holy Island on the Northumbrian coast, the southern march includes Wooler, Alwinton, Elsdon, Bellingham, Newcastleton, Langholm, Eskdalemuir, Ettrick Forest and Moffat to Tweedsmuir;. the western march from Tweedsmuir is via Tweeddale and Eddlestone Water; whilst the northern march follows the Moorfoot/Lammermuir fault to the North Sea by Cockburnspath. The North Sea coast closes the net. This net of myth and magic stretches some 75 miles (120km) east to west and 50 miles (80km) north to south, and includes country inns and village pubs that mirror the character of Border life and replenish the spirit of the Border traveller.

This guide is not a judgement on those establishments included in or excluded from the guide, it is simply a collection of what I sincerely hope are useful suggestions and aids for those who love the great outdoors. Many fine and well run pubs have not been included purely and simply on the grounds of their location and a dearth of public paths, as experienced in the larger towns and intensive agricultural areas. Or, as in the case of ideally situated inns, establishments may have lost some of their former appeal.

All establishments included in this publication are aware of the author's intentions.

A GUIDE TO THE GUIDE

Aims

To locate and identify the inn by number, map, grid reference, description and photograph/illustration.

To describe comprehensively and objectively all aspects of the establishment that influence the customer, particularly those of the outdoor persuasion.

To link the pub with items of local interest and attainable, enjoyable local walks.

Layout

Chapters 1 to 4 contain details of 53 inns/pubs. Chapter 1 covers 16 pubs in the northern confines of Northumberland, Chapter 2 plots the course of 18 inns in the eastern half of the Scottish Borders, whilst Chapter 3 traces 15 hostelries into the higher, wilder western half of the Scottish Borders. The pubs in each chapter are numbered geographically, ie. from east to west for each of the three areas, based on the old walker's logic that it is wise to travel with the sun.

Chapter 4 lists four outstanding or unusual howffs on the approaches to the Borders where the traveller, from Edinburgh, Glasgow and the Central Belt or Tyneside, can pause awhile and contemplate the mysteries and delights ahead.

A simple map of the area pin-points the location of each inn by number. In each chapter the inn/pub is identified by name, address and telephone/fax number, followed by its situation with map reference and access details. A general description, physical and atmospheric, is followed by a complete "CV" of uncluttered facts relating to everything outdoor travellers require. Finally there are details highlighting food, items of local interest and walks with photographs or illustrations.

ACCESS

Air Links: National and International flights through Glasgow, Edinburgh and Newcastle Airports.

Rail Links: East coast inter-city stopping at Berwick-upon-Tweed; west coast inter-city stopping at Carlisle (connecting with Scottish Borders Rail Link bus). Local stopping trains supplement this service from Tyneside, Edinburgh and Glasgow.

Road Links: A1(M) north to Tyneside; from Tyneside north, A1 to Berwick-upon-Tweed, A697 to Wooler and Coldstream, A68 to Jedburgh. From Hexham B6320 to Bellingham, from Carlisle A7 to Langholm.

From Edinburgh south, A1 to Berwick-upon-Tweed, A68 to Lauder, A7 to Galashiels, A703 to Peebles. From Glasgow south-east, A74 to Moffat, A73(T) and A721 via Carnwath and A72 to Peebles.

Bus Services: Long Distance City Link services pass through the Borders.

Local Services: Towns and villages have connecting services, supplemented by the Post Bus service.

Timetables etc. available at stations and TICs.

"WALKER'S PUB CODE" OR "WHA'S FUU NOO"

To assist those not too familiar with the Border inn. Whilst not prescribing to the "Thou shalt not do" doctrine, I do subscribe to common sense and courtesy in matters inebriant as in matters pedestrian.

DO REMOVE	your sodden boots before entering a carpeted bar.
DO REMOVE	dripping outer garments.
DO REMOVE	sacs. Big sacs in small bars make poor companions.
DO RESIST	nursing your $^1/_2$ pint for $2^1/_2$ hours in the fireside chair.
DO RESIST	shouting on entering "A pint of your best wallop, Landlord".
DO REMEMBER	if you are a large party to advise the pub of your numbers and estimated time of arrival.
DO REMEMBER	to clear it with the landlord that it's OK to leave your car in the car park before you disappear over the nearest Corbett for 6 hours; and to leave your Route Directions.
DO REMEMBER	to compliment the landlord/staff on the good things you have enjoyed.
DO REMEMBER	that the beer mats, beer towels, toilet rolls, pictures and memorabilia all belong to the publican.

* * *

ADVICE TO READERS

Readers are advised that whilst every effort is taken by the author to ensure the accuracy of this guidebook, changes can occur which may affect the contents. New fences and stiles appear, waymarking alters, there may be new buildings or eradication of old buildings. It is advisable to check locally on transport, accommodation, shops etc. Even rights of way can be altered, paths can be eradicated by landslip, forest clearances or changes of ownership. The publisher would welcome notes of any such changes.

LEGEND

Symbol	Meaning	Symbol	Meaning
●	Pub/Inn		Sea or loch shore
• • • •	Walks route		Sea cliffs/rocks
✣	Abbey/church		River
	Ruin of abbey/ church		Pre-historic fort/ settlement
	Border		Conifers
▲	Summit		Broad leaved trees
	Cairn	▬ ▬ ▬	Hall's wall

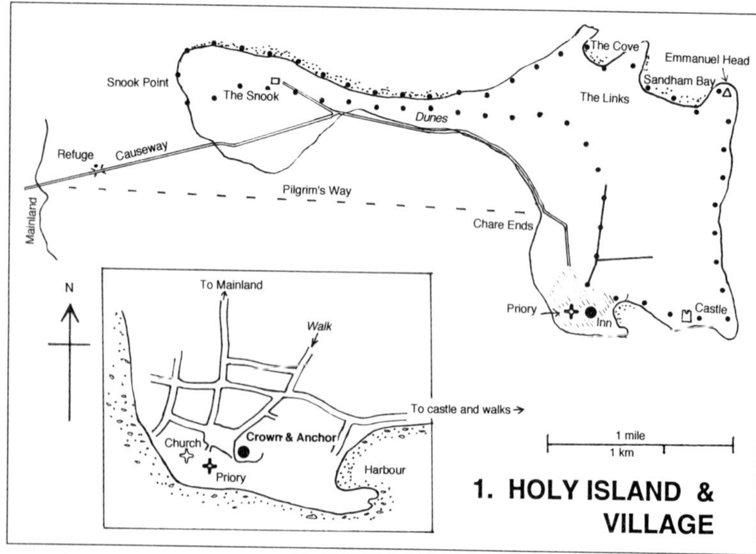

1. HOLY ISLAND & VILLAGE

Chapter 1
Northumbrian Borders

HOLY ISLAND *(LINDISFARNE)*

1. CROWN AND ANCHOR INN - Holy Island, Berwick-upon-Tweed, Northumberland TD15 2RX. (01289) 89215 (389215 from 30th January 1995) ***Colour photo opposite p32***

Holy Island, an island twice every 24 hours, is anchored to the coast by a causeway; 5 miles (8km) east of the A1(T) road at GR 053421, 10 miles (16km) south of Berwick-upon-Tweed. The Crown and Anchor stands by the Priory, looking out to sea.

SITUATION *OS Map Landranger.Sheet 751:50,000 GR 126419*

TIDE TABLES ARE PROMINENTLY DISPLAYED ON NOTICE BOARDS.

A century ago the island supported 300 inhabitants, and they in turn supported at least 10 inns, opening at 6am. The Crown and Anchor survives, with its distinctive white walls overlooking the Harbour (quaintly called The Ooze) and the Castle. Records trace it back to 1835, when the landlord kept a pony and trap for carting visitors to and from the island at low tide. A tradition carried on by the high-clearance Model-T Ford before the present causeway was built.

Three rooms, displaying seascape prints, creels and a boxed-fox provide sustenance for the visitor. The cheerful bar with its red-brick fireplace and overhead dinghy, where many visitors trip in/out via the "bad-step", is the most spacious and understandably the most popular. A comfortable No-Smoking lounge and dining room lead from the bar and the hotel entrance, in this local with the happy atmosphere.

OPEN:	December to February, 12 noon-3pm, 7-11pm March to November, 11am-3pm, 7-11pm
TYPE:	Free House
ON DRAUGHT:	Jennings Bitter, Websters Yorkshire Bitter, Websters Best Murphy's Irish Stout, Carlsberg Lager, Strongbow Cider
BOTTLED:	Newcastle Brown Ale, Carlsberg Special Brew, plus a selection of beers, stout, lager and cider
WHISKY:	Proprietary blends, Irish, de-luxe and 21 malts

WINE:	White, vin de pays on tap; red. Increasing wine list of "in-demand" choices
FOOD:	Lunch-time only, a flexible 12 noon-2-ish pm. Daily specials blackboard plus menu served in the bar, lounge and dining area
ACCOMMODATION:	3 double, 2 en-suite, 1 public facilities. Heated
FACILITIES:	Beer garden with picnic tables. Bar darts, dominoes, cards, solitaire and occasional TV
OPEN FIRES:	Bar and lounge bar/dining room
WALKERS:	Welcome, as are all outdoor enthusiasts
CHILDREN:	Welcome as the swallows - during summer
DOGS:	No
PARKING:	Limited to 5; public car parks close by

FOOD

As one would expect sea-food is a feature, together with a wide variety of healthy, home-grown salad dishes. Not forgetting the home-cooked hams and beefs; chips rarely appear. Sandwiches and rolls available with home-made fillings. Don't miss the crab.

ITEMS OF LOCAL INTEREST

Founded in AD635 by St Aiden, Lindisfarne Priory is a cradle of Christianity. An annual pilgrimage follows the posted "Pilgrim's Way" across Holy Island Sands via the Chare Ends, to the Priory.

Dry-shod o'er sands, twice every day,
The pilgrims to the shrine find way:
Twice every day, the waves efface
Of staves and sandall'd feet the trace.

Visit Lindisfarne Castle, circa 1550, restored by Lutyens in 1930; and the entire island, an English Nature, National Nature Reserve. Famous for wintering and breeding waterfowl and shorebirds.

WALKS

A 9 mile (14.4km) coastal adventure, best taken when Holy Island is so.

Walk E to the inverted Coble shells, Lutyens "walnut whip" castle and limekilns on Beblowe crag. Swing N on coastline for 1 mile (1.6km) by Sheldrake Point, Brides Hole to the white Pyramid at Emmanuel Head. Spectacular views of two castles, priory and the scattered Farne Islands. Descend W to Sandham Bay then the "bird-washed" cliffs of Cove Haven (care on the cliff rim). Pass Snipe Point and Back Skerrs to the sandy North Shore stretching SW/W for 2½ miles (4km) to Snook Point, the western extremity of the island. U-turn left into the grassy dunes to Snook House, continue E on the inland shank over The Links (old golf course) to meet a farm track 1 mile (1.6km) N of the Crown and Anchor.

BERWICK UPON TWEED

2. PILOT INN - Low Greens, Berwick upon Tweed, Northumberland TD15 1LZ. (01289) 304124

The historic walled town of Berwick-upon-Tweed, now by-passed by the A1(T), is 60 miles (96km) north of Newcastle and 60 miles south-east of Edinburgh. Low Greens runs east from Castlegate (opposite the Castle Hotel), with the Pilot Inn on the north side.

SITUATION *OS Map Landranger: Sheet 75 1:50,000 GR 997534*

Berwick's picturesque "Greenses" harbour and the community of Low Greens was, in years gone by, the centre of a thriving fishing industry. Sadly little remains today but memories, no cobles grace the harbour and only the Pilot Inn is left of the three inns listed in 1855. Originally tied to Coldstream Brewery, this two storied pub with its solid sandstone walls is now the "gable-ender" to

Berwick-upon-Tweed - Pilot Inn

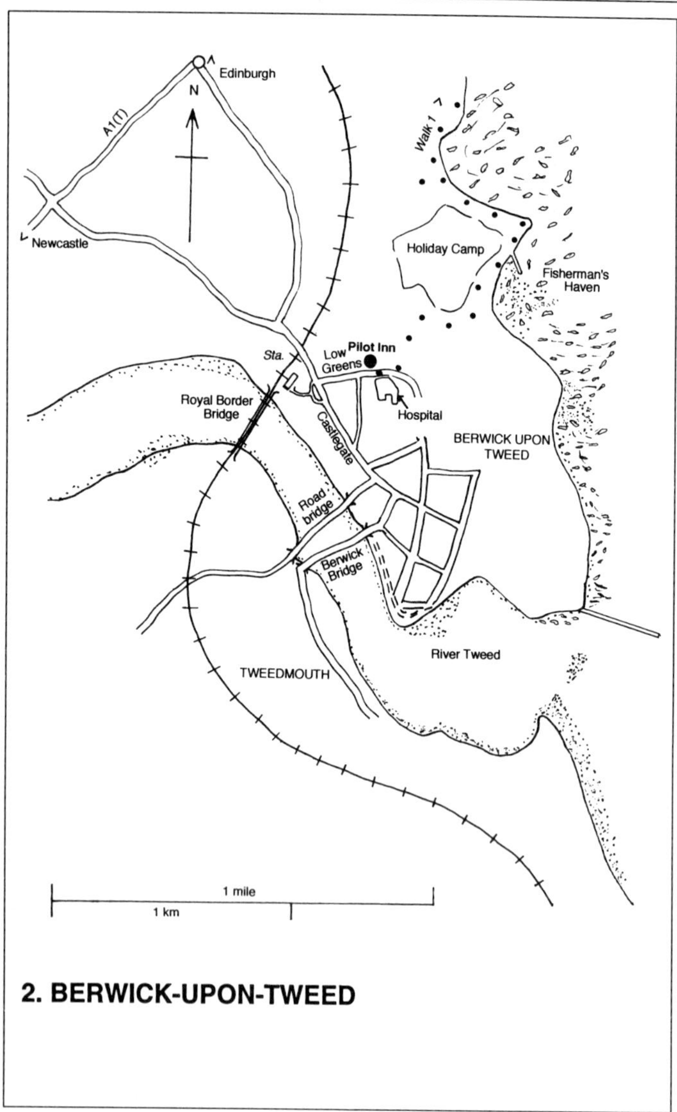

2. BERWICK-UPON-TWEED

a row of fisher-folk cottages. Enlarged and extended in 1916 (see the guttering) from a single bar, it thankfully remains a fishing-folk local. The entrance hall and passage floors inlaid with fan-patterned mosaics (by Italian POWs), the beamed bar cheerfully festooned with fishing memorabilia, ships in bottles, fading photos of Greenses folk and "Walker's Logs". A delightful bar, with a fine selection of well kept beers on the mahogany counter, and an eye-pleasing yellow American pine fireplace. Three lounge bars, also repositories for nautical spares, retain the character of the inn, making this local a "hands on'" experience of old Greenses.

OPEN:	Summer	(Easter to October), 11am-3pm, 7-11pm
	Winter	Monday-Thursday, 12 noon-2pm, 8-11pm
		Friday-Saturday, 11am-3pm, 7-11pm
		Sunday, 12 noon-3pm, 7-10.30pm
TYPE:	Free House	
ON DRAUGHT:	Federation Special Ale, Newcastle Exhibition, Theakston B B, Stones Best Bitter, Younger's Tartan Special, Federation Pale Ale, Murphy's Irish Stout, Federation LCL Lager - beware do not over indulge, Tennent's Lager	
BOTTLED:	Becks Bier, Guinness and selection of stouts, Carlsberg Special Brew and ciders including Diamond White	
WHISKY:	Proprietary blends and two malts	
WINE:	House white, dry and medium; red	
FOOD:	Soup, sandwiches and snacks only	
ACCOMMODATION:	No	
FACILITIES:	Darts and dominoes	
OPEN FIRES:	Gas fires in the bar and lounge bars	
WALKERS:	Welcome, landlord is an enthusiast	
CHILDREN:	No	
DOGS:	No	
PARKING:	Kerbside in the street	

ITEMS OF LOCAL INTEREST

In its hey-day Low Greens and Greenses saw 36 cobles sail from Fisherman's Haven. The locality was also somewhat of a "No-Go" area, where the attraction of unlicensed salmon was always compulsive; the unwary stranger was frequently mistaken for a bailiff/debt collector - stoned first and questioned later. Berwick itself, up to the late 1200s, was an ancient and important Scottish seaport. Then the wars began, and in two centuries of conflict the town changed hands 14 times, finishing in England's camp in 1482. Two road bridges span the Tweed, the old bridge 1634, the new bridge 1928; and Robert Stephenson's Royal Border rail bridge 1850.

WALKS

An exhilarating 6¾ miles (11km), time 3 hours, via precipitous cliffs and black coves to Burnmouth. Walk E from the Pilot via the golf course to a holiday centre above Fisherman's Haven. A cliff top path zig-zags NW by Sharpers Head and Brotherstones Hole, with only the wheeling gull and the restless sea for company. Continue NNW via the stac Needles Eye to a waymarked stile into a caravan park by the cliffs of Marshall Meadows Bay. Ascend over an old bridge to follow the cliff top fence to the Scottish Border - GR 979575. Ahead lie the rearing cliffs and smugglers' coves of Tods Loup, Lamberton Skerrs and Catcairn Bushes. *Caution on the exposed paths between the railway and the vertiginous cliffs.* After a series of rocky mounds a fence/wall needs to be crossed prior to descending to Ross Farm. At the rail bridge turn right with the field fence, seawards to a snicket between fence/wall. A faint grassy path zig-zags steeply to the shoreline houses at Gowdrait and Burnmouth.

Two shorter circular walks, in and around Berwick, are detailed in Chapter 5, *The Border Country - A Walker's Guide* by Alan Hall.

WOOLER

3. RYECROFT HOTEL - Ryecroft Way, Wooler, Northumberland NE71 6AB. (01668) 281459/281233 Fax (01668) 282214

Wooler shelters below the eastern Cheviots, astride Wooler Water at the head of the Milfield plain; 13½ miles (21.6km) south of Coldstream, 16½ miles (26.4km) north-west of Alnwick, on the A697. The Ryecroft is in the elbow of the A697 and Ryecroft Way.

SITUATION

OS Map Landranger. Sheet 75 1:50,000 GR 992285

Wooler, a Northumbrian market town mentioned in 1254, appears to have led a quiet life for a Border frontier town, the quiet rhythms of life being ruffled only by three disastrous fires in 1693, 1722 and 1863.

The red-brick art decor style of the purpose-built Ryecroft places this friendly, family-run hotel in the 1930s. One of an exclusive pair it was not a hotel until 1946, being commandeered as an officer's mess during the 1939-46 conflict. A most comfortable carpeted hotel, with a stylish mirrored reception hall directing the visitor in all directions. The lounge bar, leading into a pleasing sun-lounge, exhibits all the trappings of the period; the counter backed by shelves, mirrors and shining bottles, the walls bearing languid lamp bearing statuettes above plush, padded wall seats. Oils, etchings and old photographs

Wooler - Ryecroft Hotel

on every wall, including an oil painting by a local artist of old "Ryecroft" in the sizeable dining room. It's not a place to walk into with muddy boots (these can be removed in the vestibule and transferred to the drying room) but it is a fine place to meet those of a like mind.

BAR OPEN: All year, 11am-3pm, 6-11pm
TYPE: Free House
ON DRAUGHT: Marston's Pedigree, Yates Bitter, Theakston Best Bitter, Exhibition 60/-, McEwan's Best Scotch, Carlsberg Lager

BOTTLED:	Newcastle Brown Ale, Guinness, Carlsberg Special Brew and a selection of beer, stouts, lager and cider
WHISKY:	Proprietary blends and selected malts
WINE:	House white, dry/medium; red. A thoughtful wine list
FOOD:	Bar-lunch, 12 noon-2pm; evening meal (dining room) 7-8.30pm
ACCOMMODATION:	4 double, 1 twin, 2 family, 2 single, all en-suite. Family annexe includes full facilities
FACILITIES:	Drying room - residents and non-residents. Dominoes
OPEN FIRES:	Lounge bar/reception hall, with brass, marble surrounds
WALKERS:	Most welcome, as are all outdoor enthusiasts. Walking holidays and weekends arranged
CHILDREN:	Welcome
DOGS:	Not in eating areas, or in proximity of resident labrador
PARKING:	Sizeable car park, walker's vehicles left by arrangement, plus route plan details.

FOOD

Home cooked, using fresh locally produced ingredients, with the emphasis on local game, fresh- and salt-water fish, the sweets a speciality of the proprietor. Daily specials are on the bar blackboard and the small evening menu is changed daily.

ITEMS OF LOCAL INTEREST

Wooler was considered as a possible termination point for the Pennine Way and remains a centre for "exploring Chevioteers". The surrounding hills yield a rich crop of prehistoric forts and "cup & ring" marks *(sculptured rings with a central cup* eg Yeavering Bell and Weetwood). Booklets on local walks are available at the Ryecroft and the TIC.

WALKS

1) A circular walk of 4¾ miles (7.6km) from Wooler, ascending 377ft (115m) onto Weetwood Moor. Cross the bridge E to Brewery Road, ascend to a signpost, continue NE to a sunken path E onto Weetwood Moor. On the moor fork right for a skyline plantation before swinging NE to more conifers, the E end of which hides two rocky outcrops with "cup & ring" marks. Clearer examples lie E marked by cairns 160yds from the road. Follow the road right to the trig point, descend S and NW to pass Coldmartin Loughs (whose water never freezes). Continue NW (ignore the metallic device) before joining the outward route from Wooler.

2) More "cup & ring" marks, a stone circle, forts and settlements can be seen over Doddington Moor and Dod Law. Walk from Doddington or

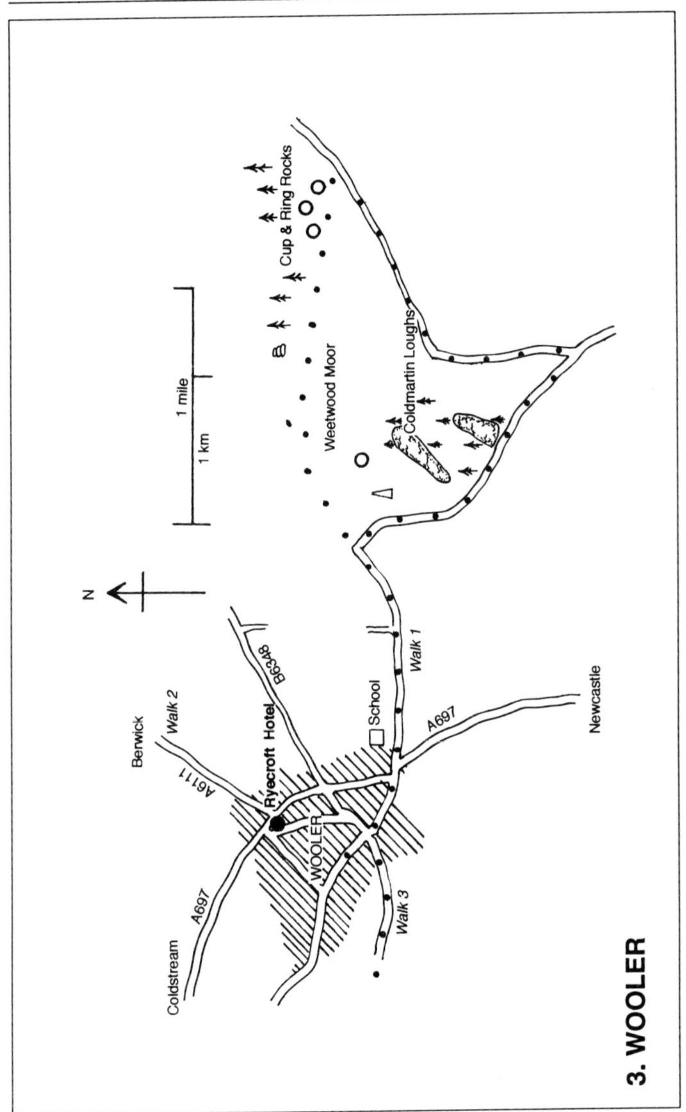
3. WOOLER
N
1 mile
1 km
Cup & Ring Rocks
Weetwood Moor
Coldmartin Loughs
Walk 1
Walk 2
Walk 3
Berwick
A6111
Ryecroft Hotel
B6348
School
A697
Newcastle
WOOLER
A697
Coldstream

Horton.

3) A 7 mile (11.2km) hike into typical Cheviot country, with no severe ascents. SW from Wooler via Ramsey Lane to Brown Law, S to Wooler Common Farm and SW on Hellpath, turning right NW beyond Watch Hill plantation to Commonburn House. Pass the house, right, onto the road which is followed E to Brown Law and Wooler.

ALLERDEAN

4. THE PLOUGH - Allerdean, Berwick upon Tweed, Northumberland TD15 2DB. (01892) 387206

On the crossroads of the B6354 Duddo to Berwick road and an unclassified road east from Norham. Marked on the OS map as West Allerdean, a village of few houses; it lies 4 miles (6.4km) south west of Berwick and 4 1/2 miles (7.2km) east of Norham.

SITUATION *OS Map Landranger. Sheet 74 1:50,000 GR 965464*

Created in the mid 1600s, this now white, bright and cheerful pub where all are welcome was an overnight stop for pilgrims bound to/from Holy Island. Named "The Folly", a local name for Safe House or Haven, it held that name until the mid 1900s. A smithy, a stable with a cobbled, channelled floor and tether rings adjoined the present pub.

A single porch door leads into a smiling cornucopia of wooden panels and exposed stone, a black beamed ceiling and a parquet floor scattered with barrel tables. The walls adorned with artifacts agricultural and brewing. To the right a large recessed stone fireplace surrounded by a small lounge bar, an eating area for families, leads into a bright, light games/pool room. To the left of the bar (watch the step) a pleasant dining room with pale pine tables and a small "no-smoking" dining room. Beyond, the kitchen, from which wafts at weekends the temptations of slow roasting border beef; accompanied by unexplained sightings of a dark haired child bobbing up outside the kitchen window.

OPEN: Weekdays/Saturday, 12 noon-3pm, 6.30-11pm
Sunday, 12 noon-3pm, 7-10.30pm

TYPE: Free House

ON DRAUGHT: Theakston Best Bitter, Marston's Pedigree Ale, Newcastle Exhibition, McEwan's Best Scotch, Younger's Tartan Special, McEwan's Lager, Strongbow Dry Cider

BOTTLED: Newcastle Brown Ale, Vaux Double Maxim, Becks Bier, a range of stouts, Carlsberg Special Brew, strong ciders

WHISKY:	Standard Proprietary blends plus a selection of 20 malts
WINE:	House wine - white, dry and medium; red; a small wine list
FOOD:	Daily 12 noon-2pm and 7-9pm. Menu and specials blackboard. Only snacks in the bar
ACCOMMODATION:	No
FACILITIES:	Pool room with darts, juke box. Dominoes, draughts, bandit and quiz machine. Children's play area, garden tables and Caravan Club certificated location
OPEN FIRES:	In the bar and an iron stove in the lounge bar
WALKERS:	Welcome. Please leave heavy/wet gear in the porch or hand it to the staff for safe keeping
CHILDREN:	Welcome in the eating and play sections
DOGS:	Allowed under control, but not in eating areas
PARKING:	At the front of the pub with an overflow available

FOOD

The home-cooked traditional specials of roast Border beef and Yorkshire

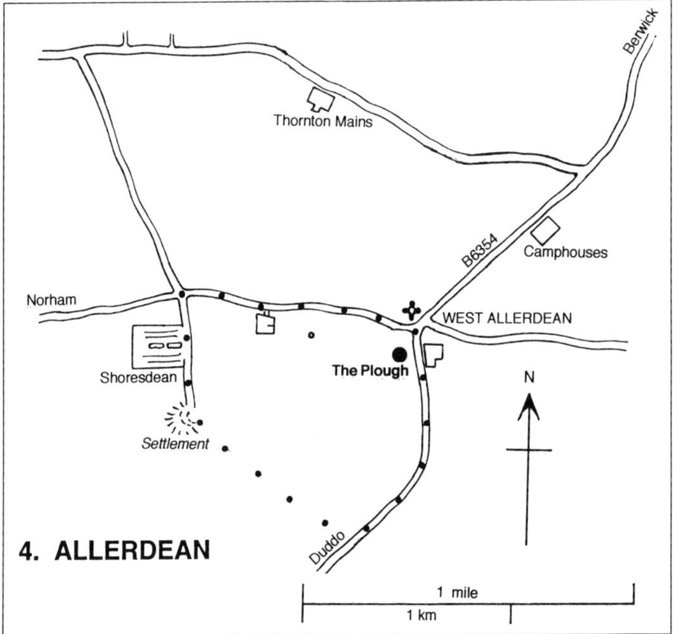

pudding, steak and ale pie, spotted dick, treacle sponge and bread pudding attract locals and visitors alike. The lasagne and home-made vegetarian dishes are also in demand. Waitress service.

ITEMS OF LOCAL INTEREST

Nearby Grindonrigg and Battle Moor both claim to be the site of the battle of Grindon Rig 1568. A battle between Sir Henry Percy's forces and a contingent of booty laden Scots returning home. Close by at Duddo a sorely decayed pele tower and a circle of standing stones. Closer to Allerdean at nearby Shoresdean an Iron Age settlement can be seen.

WALKS

W to Shoresdean then S, ie left passing the village via a cart track to the prehistoric settlement. A right of way, marked on the OS map, SW to Ancroft Northmoor, then return NW and N to Allerdean via the B6354.

An interesting walk from Duddo takes in the old pele tower and stone circle. N via the right of way footpath for 1½ miles (a detour en route W for 500yds to the stone circle) to join a country lane at GR 934446, which is then followed first left and left again turning S to Grindonrigg. Continue S through the conifers to a crossroads, turn left returning to Duddo ¾ mile (1.2km) E.

HOLYSTONE

5. THE SALMON INN - Holystone, Sharperton, Morpeth, Northumberland NE65 7AJ. (01669) 50285 (650285 from 13th December 1994)

Holystone, a delightful cluster of Northumbrian stone, lies in Upper Coquetdale 2½ miles (4km) north of the B6341 and 9½ miles (15.2km) west of Rothbury. The distinct Salmon Inn graces the north-west corner of the village.

SITUATION *OS Map Landranger. Sheet 81 1:50,000 GR 954027*

The garden hamlet of Holystone, aflame in summer, draws many foot and motorised visitors. Attracted not only by the scenic delights of Coquetdale but also by the seventeenth-century Salmon Inn, a stone-built haven of character and warmth. A pub in an area renowned for "Whiskey, Salmon, old milk cheese, barley cake and fresh butter". The "soft" climate of Coquetdale (for Lady's Well is said never to freeze) plus the friendly close beamed bar, with its splendid

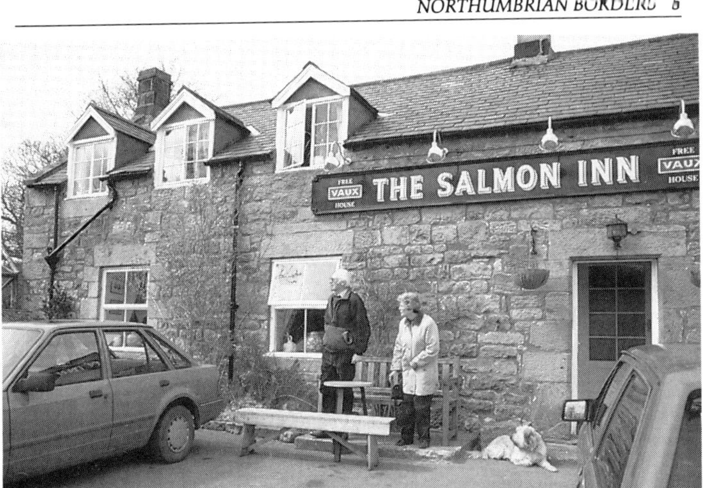

Holystone - The Salmon Inn

stone-framed open fire complete with priest's hole, so warm in winter, so visually pleasing in summer, help make the inn popular with locals and visitors. Thick walls, little windows aplenty, prints and tales upon the walls, a leaning plank on the bar counter - little wonder the ubiquitous pool table is "hoyed" out in summer to make room for folk.

The pleasant lounge bar/eating area (though most eat in the bar) is on the right when entering.

OPEN: 11am-3pm (Sundays 12 noon-3pm), 7-11pm
TYPE: Vaux Tied House
ON DRAUGHT: Vaux Samson, Lorrimer's Best Scotch, Vaux Light, Guinness, Carlsberg Export Lager, Labatt's Lager, Bulmers Original Cider, Symonds' Scrumpy Jack
BOTTLED: Double Maxim, Maxim, Carlsberg Special Brew plus a selection of beer, stout, lager and cider
WHISKY: Proprietary blends and a few malts
WINE: House white-medium; red
FOOD: Bar meals during opening hours except Sunday evenings. Waitress service and specials blackboard
ACCOMMODATION: No
FACILITIES: Pool table (winter only), bandit, dominoes, darts. Piped (Northumbrian

	that is) music, front door benches
OPEN FIRES:	Two fireplaces in the bar, one majestic live fire
WALKERS:	Welcome and encouraged
CHILDREN:	Yes, only to 9pm
DOGS:	Yes, away from food
PARKING:	Spacious parking, with overflow, at front

FOOD

The selection of pub grub may be limited, not so the quality or the quantity. Home made steak pie, with light short-crust pastry overflows the plate. Sandwiches and children's helpings available; advisable to have the walk first and make it a long one.

ITEMS OF LOCAL INTEREST

Lady's Well, a holy well enclosed in Roman times, is a clear spring of pure bright water hidden in a copse to the north of Holystone, which is used today for Holystone's water supply. It stands beside an old Roman road from Bremenium to the Devil's Causeway and the coast. In its waters the missionary Paulinus is reputed to have baptised 3,000 pagan Northumbrians in AD 627. In the fifth century, it was associated with St Ninian apostle of the Borders, and in the twelfth century a Priory for Augustinian Cannonesses was built close by.

South of Holystone there are Bronze Age burial mounds, the Five Barrows; also Mungo's Well, of which little is known.

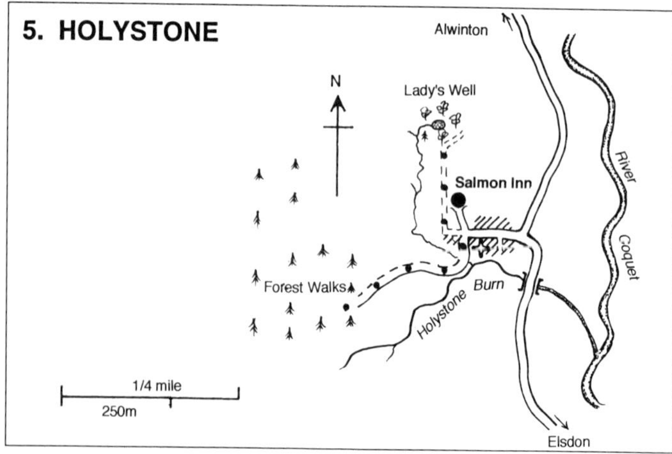

WALKS

A 1/2 mile return stroll from the Salmon to Lady's Well (which can be extented to Wood Hall), plus three varied forest walks from 1/2 mile west.

Signposted/waymarked from the forest parking/picnic area:

1) 1/2 hour Green Walk via Lady's Well and the Nunnery.
2) 1 hour Orange Walk past Old Oak Wood to Dove Crag, with a gorge return.
3) 2 1/2 hour Red Walk through the Old Beeches to Dove Crag, alternative return by open fell.

ELSDON

6. BIRD IN BUSH - Elsdon, Nr Otterburn, Northumberland NE19 1AA. (01830) 520000

Elsdon, a remote fellside village, sits astride the B6341; 3 miles (4.8km) east of Otterburn and the A696(T), 12 miles (19.2km) south-west of Rothbury. The solid grey Bird in Bush is a bastion on the north-west corner of the village green.

SITUATION *OS Map Landranger. Sheet 80 1:50,000 GR 936931*

> *Hae ye ivver been at Elsdon? The world's unfinish'd neuk;*
> *It stands amang the hungry hills An' wears a frozen leuk.*
>
> Chatt

Timeless space, light years away from the motorised bustle of the A696(T), surrounds the solid stones of Elsdon. In the 1700s three pubs serviced Elsdon, the Bacchus, the Crown and Bird in Bush; today only one remains. Overlooking the village green the Bird in Bush, circa 1781, stands secure, its front door leading to an interior of style and character. Long low rooms, a battery of beers and an immediate friendly welcome confirms this is a "canny" pub, where the maximum use of space is evident in bar and lounge capturing comfort, practicality and form. Original beams and cupboards, blown-glass lanterns, flocks of exquisite bird prints and historic artifacts provide a character personified by the child's "tackity boot" good luck charm found in the eaves.

OPEN:	*Summer:*	*Winter:*
	Weekdays, 12 noon-2pm, 7-11pm	7-11pm
	Weekends, 12 noon-3pm, 6-11pm	12 noon-3pm, 7-11pm
TYPE:	Free House	

ON DRAUGHT:	Boddingtons Bitter, Theakston BB, Newcastle Exhibition, McEwan's Best Scotch, Newcastle IPA, Guinness, Carlsberg Lager, McEwan's Lager, Dry Blackthorn Cider
BOTTLED:	Newcastle Brown Ale, McEwan's 90/- and 80/-, Maxim Light, Carlsberg Special Brew; selection of stout, lager, cider
WHISKY:	Proprietary blends, Irish, rye and malts
WINE:	3 chilled house whites, 1 red
FOOD:	Soup and sandwiches, 12 noon-2pm. Ask about evening grub
ACCOMMODATION:	No, except in dire emergencies
FACILITIES:	Beer garden. Shove ha'penny (genuine half-pennies), darts, dominoes, draughts, cribbage, local news-sheet
OPEN FIRES:	Enclosed gas fires, in bar and lounge
WALKERS:	Most welcome, but please respect the pile carpets
CHILDREN:	In the lounge only, up to 8pm
DOGS:	Welcome on the floor, as per example set by the 360lbs of 4 resident dogs
PARKING:	Street and greenside parking

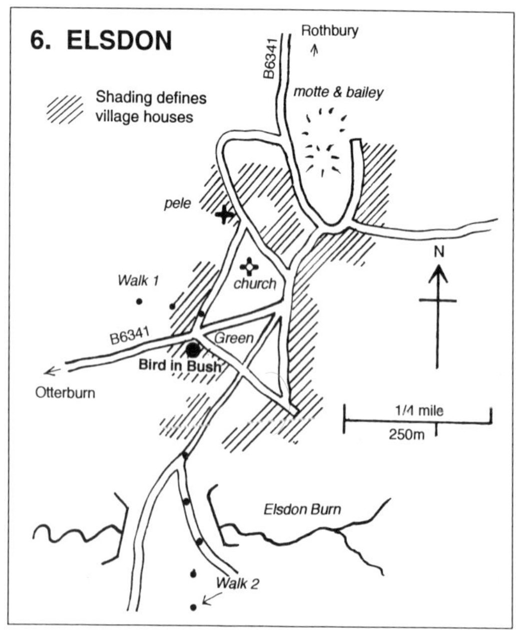

FOOD

Home-made soups with hot rolls, plus freshly prepared sandwiches/ toasties/stotties with varied fillings and salad.

ITEMS OF LOCAL INTEREST

Once capital of Redesdale, Elsdon is derived from either Ellysden - Dene of Ellers (Alders) or "elde" - old and "dun" - hill fort. The fourteenth-century parish church of St Cuthbert, the Priest's House, and what's left of the Norman "motte and bailey" castle are worth a visit. An unruly settlement populated by several "fighting families" of Halls, Hedleys and Potts, much given to reiving and cattle-lifting; described in 1618 as "Notorious, Lewde, Idle and Misbehaved Persons in Redesdale".

WALKS

1) A signposted public path leads from the green, W and NW to The Folly. After 1 mile (1.6km) at the road junction turn right onto a farm track leading NE to Dunshield, where a bridleway is joined, returning S to Elsdon alongside the tree lined banks of Elsdon Burn.

2) Leave Elsdon S, swing left at the fork and once over Elsdon Burn ascend with the public footpath and cart track to Hillhead. Continue SE on cart track and road (fine views of the valley and surrounding fells) to the gallows, complete with a macabre head, at Stengs Cross (where William Wilson was hanged in 1791). Return NW and N, by the outward lane to just beyond Todholes road end, then by public pathway to Elsdon.

Elsdon - Bird in Bush

MILFIELD

7. RED LION INN - Milfield, Wooler, Northumberland NE71 6JD. (01668) 6224 (216224 from 27th February 1995)

Milfield straddles the busy A697, below the eastern Cheviots and alongside the horseshoes of the River Till; 6½ miles (10.4km) north-west of Wooler and 9½ miles (15.2km) south-east of Coldstream. The Red Lion holds centre stage, east side of the A697.

SITUATION *OS Map Landranger. Sheet 74 1:50,000 GR 934338*

A coaching inn since the late 1700s with the name Red Lion, though one theory suggests this name is a derivation of "Red Line" (Flodden military connections - unlikely). One undisputed fact is that the inn was the 6 mile link between Crookham and Wooler for changing coach-horses on the Edinburgh-Newcastle mail route. Close by stood the forge and coach house and the saddlers; east of the inn stood old Millfield (two ls).

The rather serious exterior of this local fortunately does not filter into the bars. From the front door swing right for the public bar, left for the lounge bar; functional, friendly and cosy as a pub should be. The bar is small with a plain side door, coat rack, bar mirrors, military prints, and small round tables, allowing room to stretch, enjoy the pint and have one's crack. The lounge bar is beamed, with assorted solid tables, cushioned wall settles and a sprinkling of agricultural memorabilia and fading photographs. All give second place to the "walk-in" sandstone fireplace, with its horseshoe "Dogs", and one pillar worn smooth with sharpening steel.

OPEN:	Monday to Saturday 11.30am-3pm, 7-11pm (closed Tuesday night) Sunday, 12 noon-3pm, 7-10.30pm
TYPE:	Free House
ON DRAUGHT:	Wm McEwan 80/-, Border Old Kiln; Whitbread Poacher & Best Scotch, Murphy's Irish Stout, Heineken Lager, Bulmer Cider
BOTTLED:	Newcastle Brown Ale, Fowler's Wee Heavy, selection of stouts, Carslberg Special Brew, Carlsberg Lager, Pils Lager
WHISKY:	Proprietary blends and a small selection of malts
WINE:	House wine - white medium; red
FOOD:	Lunch and evening, last orders 1.45pm and 8.45pm, in the bar and lounge bar. Menus list a wholesome selection
ACCOMMODATION:	No, B&Bs can be arranged in the village
FACILITIES:	Pool room with juke box; bar-darts, dominoes, cards. Garden tables; quiz evenings winter months

Holy Island - Crown and Anchor Inn
Allerdean - The Plough

Etal - Black Bull
Falstone - The Blackcock Inn

OPEN FIRES:	Small fireplace in bar, the large fire in the lounge bar makes ones eyes water if the wind is in the wrong direction
WALKERS:	Welcome, as are cyclists
CHILDREN:	Welcome
DOGS:	On the lead and not in eating area
PARKING:	Car park at the rear, cars left by arrangement

FOOD

Local produce, be it flesh or vegetable, is used whenever possible and cooked on the premises. In great demand are the special steak and ale pie, and sausage, egg, baked beans with chips. The chips are locally praised. The menu carries sandwiches, starter snacks, six main dishes, plus vegetarian dishes (prepared at nearby Etal), ending with calorie-loaded puddings.

ITEMS OF LOCAL INTEREST

Milfield plain to the east, a wide and fertile land, was once covered by a shallow lake. Through the village runs the "ill rode", where a band of marauding Scots under Lord Hume were ambushed by English archers; the date, 1513, three weeks prior to the killing fields of Flodden.

Two miles south-west, above the narrow Glen Valley, stood the timber palace of King Edwin 616-33, the "ad Gefrin" of Bede's *Ecclesiastical History*. A roadside plaque tells of its history.

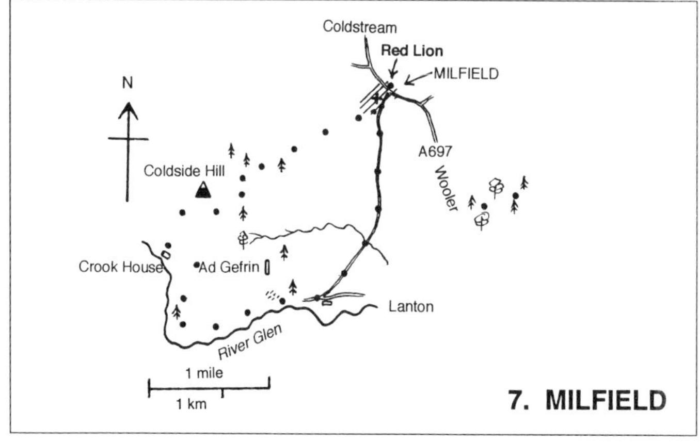

Milfield - Red Lion Inn

WALKS

A pleasing circular walk, 6 miles (9.6km), ascent 508ft (155m) time $2^{1}/_{2}$-3 hours; circles "ad Gefrin" with close-ups of the Cheviots and the dales of Bowmont, College and Glen. Leave the inn SW, via the church, to the sign "Crookhouse $2^{1}/_{2}$ miles"; turn right between football pitch/farm. After $1^{1}/_{2}$ miles (2.4km), at the second plantation, swing S between crumbling stone walls to a finger of trees, then sharp right (SW) with the stone dyke below Coldside Hill. Prior to a wall junction turn right (N) to a cart track into the Glen Valley at Crookhouse. Mouth-watering views of Yeavering Bell, Newton Tors, The Schil and Cheviot. From Crookhouse a lane winds S and E, contours the hills and follows the glen to Lanton Mill (by old Langeton Village) and the tidy steading of Lanton; fork NE and N for Milfield.

HORNCLIFFE

8. FISHERS ARMS - Main Street, Horncliffe, by Berwick-upon-Tweed, Northumberland. (01289) 386223

Horncliffe, a small village on the south bank of the River Tweed, lies 4 miles (6.4km) north-east of Norham via a minor road, and 4 miles (6.4km) west from Berwick-upon-Tweed on a minor road and the A698. The Fishers Arms is in the main street.

SITUATION *OS Map Landranger. Sheet 74 1:50,000 GR 928498*
Horncliffe, an attractive village, stands secure on a cliff of warm sandstone high above the River Tweed. Wedged tight between red sandstone houses, the Fishers Arms, one door and five windows bright with flowers, extends a cheerful welcome. As the name suggests, it provided the same welcome to the net-fishers, men who laboured hard catching salmon on the sweeping bends of the queen of rivers. Two to

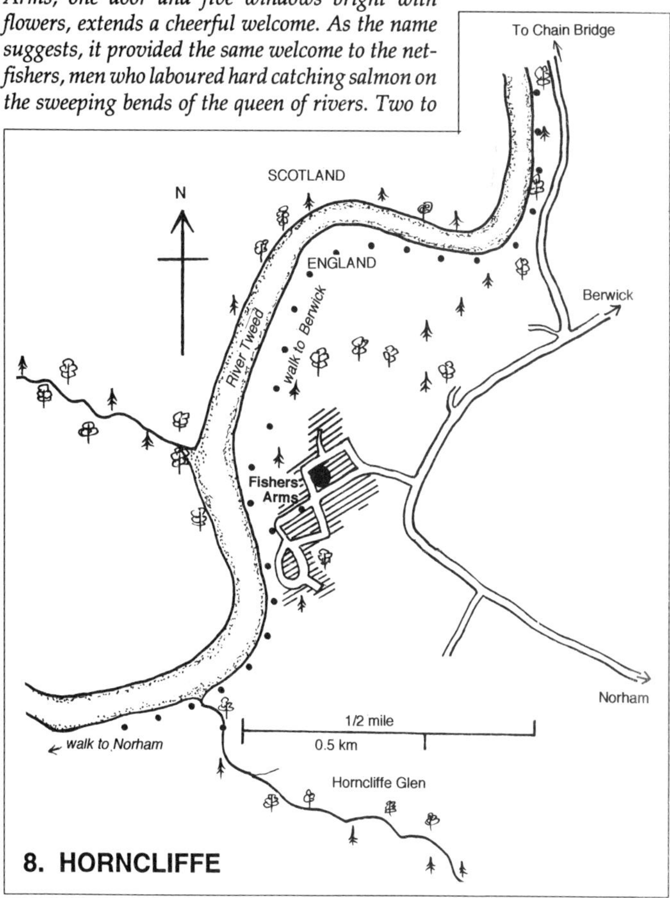

Horncliffe - Fishers Arms

three paces from the street and the visitor is in the centre of the open plan bar and lounge bar, its walls lined with covered settles and peppered with paintings/ photographs from the past. Space, which is at a premium, is well used and adds to the atmosphere in this stone-walled, coal-fired pub where the drinks selection, including wine, is complemented by a good menu of pub grub. A pub for locals and visitors.

OPEN:	Weekdays, 11am-3pm, 6.30-11pm Sunday, 12 noon-3pm, 7-10.30pm
TYPE:	Vaux House
ON DRAUGHT:	Wards Sheffield Bitter, Lorrimer's Best Scotch, Murphy's Stout, Heineken, Tuborg & Labatt's Lager
BOTTLED:	Double Maxim, Carlsberg Special Brew, plus a selection of beers, stout, lager and cider
WHISKY:	Proprietary blends
WINES:	4 house wines, plus a varied list of 12-15
FOOD:	Lunch and evening, daily specials on blackboard
ACCOMMODATION:	2 twin, one en-suite, 1 single, shared bathroom/toilet
FACILITIES:	Pool room with children's games. Darts and bandit. Quoits in summer. Background music
OPEN FIRES:	Stone fireplace in lounge

WALKERS: Most welcome
CHILDREN: Welcome in the lounge bar and pool room
DOGS: On a lead, but not near food
PARKING: Limited to the village street

FOOD
As befits its title Fishers Arms, fish, both fresh-water and salt-water, figures on the menu. A traditional menu that includes vegetarian choices and children's dishes. Service is swift with long-distance walker's appetites catered for.

ITEMS OF LOCAL INTEREST
The location of Horncliffe and its close proximity to strife-torn Berwick-upon-Tweed and Norham castle provides a rich historical mix. In 1639 the army of Charles I lay encamped by the river, and later Cromwell was to occupy a village cottage, whilst his army camped nearby.

1 1/4 miles (2km) north the Union Bridge (the Chain Bridge) spans the Tweed into Scotland. Using a wrought-iron link, which he patented in 1817, Captain Samuel Brown built this bridge in 1820. The earliest suspension bridge in Britain, and still in use today, "Vis Unitas Fortior".

WALKS
An extensive riverside footpath of 9 miles (14.4km) sweeps with the southern riverbank from the historic Border town of Berwick-upon-Tweed to the regal remains of Norham castle. Passing along the way, recently restored Paxton House on the north bank, the Union Bridge, crumbling bothies of net-fishers, Horncliffe Glen and Hangman's Land. During the summer months the path from Horncliffe to Norham can become overgrown with lush vegetation. The permutations/variations of this fascinating walk are myriad, of particular interest is the path into Horncliffe glen with its water-powered corn mill.

ETAL

9. THE BLACK BULL - Etal, Cornhill-on-Tweed, Northumberland, TD12 4TL. (01890) 820200 ***Colour photo opposite p33***
Etal (Ee-tll), a village of charm, with its castle, manor house and, a rarity in the Borders, thatched cottages, graces the B6354 10 miles (16km) south west of Berwick-upon-Tweed and 11 miles (17.6km) north of Wooler.

SITUATION *OS Map Landranger. Sheet 74 1: 50,000 GR 926394*
Alongside slated white-washed cottages, The Black Bull with its cream washed walls, thick thatch and colourful inn-sign invites the visitor to stop awhile. There has been a pub on this site for the last 250 years; old stables and a cobbled yard suggest a coaching connection, though all was lost in a disastrous fire in 1980. Thankfully the thatch was restored and the interior enlarged. A porch at the front door leads into one long narrow interior, sub-divided into the bar and the lounge bar by steps and a raised floor. "Spanish plastered" walls, liberally sprinkled with rural prints and sepia photographs of old Etal and the old Black Bull, support a low-beamed ceiling, under which a wooden bar counter glistens below the lantern lampshades. Tables and windsor chairs aplenty cover the carpeted floor. Find the brass plate stating "Take notice that as from today's date, Poachers shall be shot on first sight and if practicable questioned afterwards etc; 1868". As to its authenticity no one will comment!

OPEN:	Summer, 12 noon-3pm, 6-11pm Winter, 12 noon-2pm, 7-11pm
TYPE:	Vaux Tied House
ON DRAUGHT:	Vaux Samson Bitter, Lorrimer's Best Scotch, Guinness, Carlsberg Lager, Tuborg Lager, Heineken Lager, Symonds' Scrumpy Jack Cider
BOTTLED:	Double Maxim, Maxim, Lorrimers Export, Carlsberg Special Brew, Carlsberg Lager, Norseman Lager, Jubilee Stout
WHISKY:	Proprietary blends plus 1 malt
WINE:	House wine - white, dry and medium; red
FOOD:	Served in the lounge bar. Lunch-time to 2pm, evenings to 8.30pm. Appropriate menus midday and evening
ACCOMMODATION:	No
FACILITIES:	Bar games - darts, dominoes, cribbage and a bandit. At the front entrance trestle picnic tables and a quoits green
OPEN FIRES:	One at each gable end, set in large stone fireplaces
WALKERS:	Welcome
CHILDREN:	Welcome for food in eating area up to 8pm
DOGS:	Yes, if under control and not in eating area
PARKING:	Small car park at front, plus another 50yds east. Cars may be left with landlord's consent

FOOD
Honest to goodness pub fare, using local produce where possible, from six varying fillings for rolls/stotties, to Tweed salmon and farm-cured ham. Ten main dishes, plus children's helpings, vegetarian and vegan dishes.

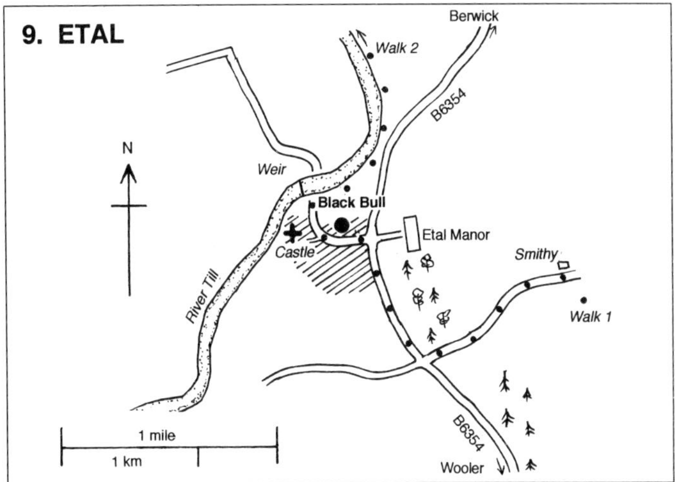

ITEMS OF LOCAL INTEREST

Etal Castle, a thirteenth-century stronghold now "gretly decaied" is at the west end; to the east a charming eighteenth-century Manor House has replaced the castle as the manor seat. The nearby Heatherslaw Water Mill, rebuilt 1806 on the site of a thirteenth-century mill, now sells the various flours etc that are produced. A narrow-gauge steam railway winds along the River Till from Heatherslaw to Etal. Ford village with its castle (Flodden connections), seventh-century church and murals by Louisa Lady Waterford is $2^{1}/_{2}$ miles south.

WALKS

1) A circular walk of $3^{3}/_{4}$ miles (6km), Etal - Errol Smithy - Hay Farm - Ford - Heatherslaw Mill - by steam train to Etal. The walk, rich in wildlife, Border history and scenery takes 2-$2^{1}/_{2}$ hours along waymarked country ways. If the train is missed, Etal is $^{3}/_{4}$ mile (1.2km) N via the road.

2) A pleasant linear riverside walk of 2 miles (3.2km) where an abundance of riverside wildlife can be enjoyed. From the Black Bull W descending to the river. Right, via an electrical installation, to a riverside path (note the herons). After 1 mile (1.6km) a swaying suspension footbridge can be crossed and the west bank explored. Return by the outward path.

Walks leaflets (varying lengths) are available at Heatherslaw Mill shop.

ALWINTON

10. ROSE AND THISTLE - Alwinton, Rothbury, Northumberland NE65 7BQ. (01669) 50226 (650226 from 13th February 1995)
The remote hamlet of Alwinton nestles beneath the southern slopes of the Cheviot Hills in upper Coquetdale; 24 miles (38.4km) south west of Wooler and 9 miles (14.4km) north-west of Rothbury. Stone-built, the Rose and Thistle is at the village's centre.

SITUATION *OS Map Landranger. Sheet 80 1:50,000 GR 920063*
Alwinton, once known as "Allenton" and still pronounced so, is as yet untouched by modern tourism. Home to the Rose and Thistle, an unpretentious pub that has been in the present landlord's family since 1907. The name is said to have come from an earlier landlord's habit of displaying a thistle when visited by "drouthy" Scots, and a rose when serving the thirsty English. Built in three sections, the east section was the original Ale House bar, and the old stable the present bar; a room that is functional, beamed above and linoed beneath, and much frequented by 'herds and those of the walking persuasion. Its walls bear little but a monster fish, a certificate qualifying our hosts to "Honorary Membership of the Fell Rescue Team", and a warning that "Smokers will be

Alwinton - Rose and Thistle

Severely Battered about the Head and Body". A larger garden bar, glass french windows et al for summer use, faces south. In 1971 the old bar was flooded, but with no burst pipes or open taps; two weeks later the poltergeist called again, overturning a heavy rocking chair.

OPEN:	Summer,	Monday to Saturday,	12 noon-11pm,
		Sunday,	12 noon-3pm, 7-11pm
	Winter,	Monday to Thursday	7-11pm
		Friday to Sunday,	12 noon-3pm, 7-11pm
TYPE:	Free House		
ON DRAUGHT:	Newcastle Exhibition, Newcastle I.P.A., McEwan's Best Scotch, Carlsberg Lager, Woodpecker Cider		
BOTTLED:	Newcastle Brown Ale, Becks Bier, Guinness, Carlsberg Special Brew, Holsten Pils plus selection of standards		
WHISKY:	Proprietary blends and various malts		
WINE:	House white, dry and medium		
FOOD:	No, only crisps, nuts and chocolates etc.		
ACCOMMODATION:	No		
FACILITIES:	Pool, darts, dominoes, bandit, juke box; garden seats		
OPEN FIRES:	No		
WALKERS:	Welcome, as are all lovers of the countryside		
CHILDREN:	Welcome		
DOGS:	Yes		
PARKING:	Free public car park 150yds west		

ITEMS OF LOCAL INTEREST

Alwinton, at the confluence of the Alwin ("White River") and the Coquet, has an interesting church built on sloping ground; its twelfth century-chancel stands ten steps above the nave and 13 above the altar. In the thirteenth to seventeenth centuries the landowners, Newminster Abbey, found it prudent to lease upper Coquetdale to local shepherds, men inclined to repel the Scottish reivers and also indulge in a little retaliation. Today, the Alwinton Shepherds' Show, a competition of a more gentle nature, is on the 2nd Saturday in October when Border sheep are shown and judged, with sheep dog trials, races, wrestling and hound trails.

WALKS

Many fine Cheviot walks surround Alwinton (avoid MOD land W and SW).

An invigorating high-level journey of 4½ hours covering 8 miles

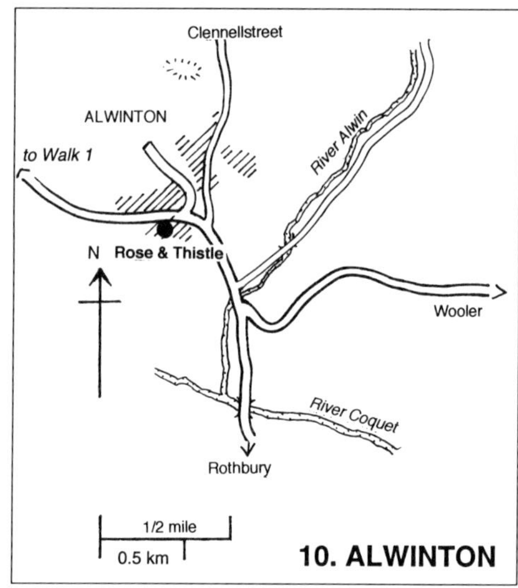

(12.8km), ascending 1214ft (370m) from the junction of Coquet and Row-hope Burns - GR 859114, to the windswept summit of Windy Gyle, 2032ft (619m).

Tight between encroaching hills the road passes the lonely steadings of Rowhope and Trows. N of Trows fork left, ascending with the waving grasses, passing conifers to the path at Little Ward Law. A mile (1.6km) NW is Windy Gyle, from whose cairned summit the Southern Uplands and the English Lakes are seen. Descend W with the Pennine Way for 2 miles (3.2km) to The Street, marked by a solitary rock at the angled fence below Mozie Law. Continue S with The Street, along a scenic grassy ridge over Black Braes and Hindside Knowe, descending steeply E to Trowhope and Coquet Water.

CROOKHAM

11. BLUEBELL INN - Pallinsburn, Crookham, Cornhill-on-Tweed, Northumberland TD12 4SH. (01890) 820252

The hamlet of Crookham shelters alongside the junction of the busy A697 and the B6353. West of the A697 the Bluebell Inn overlooks Crookham; 10½ miles (16.8km) north of Wooler, 5 miles (8km) south-east of Coldstream.

SITUATION *OS Map Landranger. Sheet 74 1:50,000 GR 910383*

In the early 1500s unnamed buildings were on this site; later documents chronicled "Blue Bell" farm, which in turn became an Ale House. In 1814 the

Crookham - Bluebell Inn

property was licenced as the Blue Bell (two words) Inn, a Royal Mail coaching inn (with its own "Blue Bell, Crookham" frank). In the 1800s the third floor was used as a dormitory for passing cattle drovers, the cots and walls scored with details of their charges and destinations. Sadly the ravages of time and the insensitivity of the brewers have changed much; the Caithness stone slabs from the bar, the drovers cots, have all gone and the name is now Bluebell (one word). Yet the cobbled-together remains still exude a welcome. The interior is cosy, the staff most kind, plus the beer from the original brick vaulted cellar is worth walking a few miles for. The narrow sectioned interior includes a lino floored bright bar, with games room leading off, a central and comfortable lounge bar with a neat and tidy dining area and an outsize "ladies" completing the decor.

OPEN:	Every day, 12 noon-3pm, 6-11pm
TYPE:	Tied House for drinks, S & N and Bass
ON DRAUGHT:	Wm McEwan 80/-, McEwan's 70/-, Theakston B B, Younger's Tartan Special, Guinness, McEwan's Lager, Symonds' Scrumpy Jack Cider
BOTTLED:	Newcastle Brown Ale, Carlsberg Special plus a selection of stout, lager and cider
WHISKY:	Proprietary blends plus a selection of 8 malts
WINE:	House wine - white, dry, medium, sweet; red. Wine list of the more popular wines
FOOD:	Bar lunches, 12 noon-2pm. Evening meals in the dining area, 7pm-9pm. Traditional roast beef Sunday 12 noon-2pm. No food on Mondays - except Bank Holidays

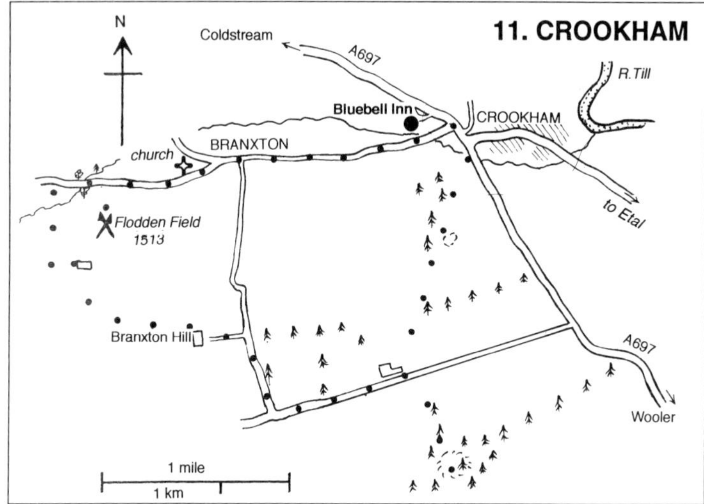

ACCOMMODATION:	No
FACILITIES:	Log seats, trestle tables front and back. Darts, dominoes, cards, cribbage, bandit; pool and quiz evenings in winter. Music night 1st Sunday each month
OPEN FIRES:	No real ones
WALKERS:	Most welcome
CHILDREN:	Welcome in the eating areas
DOGS:	No dogs
PARKING:	On the inn's frontage. Cars left with landlord's consent

FOOD

Home cooked, using local ingredients whenever possible, the snacks and meals are most satisfying. The evening meal specials of Border beef, lamb, swine, chicken and fish provide that little bit extra, whilst still catering for the vegetarian.

ITEMS OF LOCAL INTEREST

A visit to the blood stained field of Flodden (a dreich September day in 1513) by the village of Branxton, 1½ miles (2.4km) west of the inn, is not to be passed by. Norman in origin the small Church of St Paul's, Branxton, housed the body of James 1V after the battle. Note also the "Concrete Menagerie" in the village.

WALKS

A 6 mile (9.6km) circular walk via Flodden Field will delight walkers and military historians. 600yds S on the A697 turn right onto the rising path over tree-clad slopes on Pace Hill, Stanley's platform for the final stages of the battle. Continue S for 1/2 mile (0.8km) on a track to the Blinkbonny road junction below conifer-capped Flodden Hill, the Scots encampment. Turn right, ie. W, for 3/4 mile (1.2km). Prior to Branxton Moor swing N for Branxton ridge and Branxton Hill farm, battle positions of the Scots. Pass through the small gate at the farmhouse, turning left and right before descending, on a farm track, the steep slope to the ruin of Branxton Stead, slopes that proved fatal to the Scots as they stormed the English on Pipers Hill. Once past Branxton Stead note the burn prior to the road, this boggy area witnessed the greatest slaughter. From Branxton road turn right to visit Pipers Hill with its information board. The Bluebell is 1 3/4 miles (2.8km) E along the lane.

BELLINGHAM

Bellingham, the "capital" and market town of North Tynedale, flanks the north bank of the North Tyne; 9 miles (14.4km) south west of Otterburn via the B6320 and 11 miles (17.6km) east of Kielder Water reservoir.

SITUATION *OS Map Landranger. Sheet 80 1:50,000 GR 840833*

ITEMS OF LOCAL INTEREST

Bellingham (pronounced Bel-lin-jam) is a frontier town of yesteryear where even the stocky towerless parish church of St Cuthbert, AD 1180, reflects that this was not a peaceful place in medieval times. Heavily buttressed walls of extraordinary width, tiny windows widely splayed inside and a roof of stone slabs all indicate defence; an essential, for visits from the northern neighbours were seldom social.

To the north the Pennine Way fringes the cairned summit of Padon Hill, site of the "Preachings" of Sandy Peden the Scottish Covenanter, driven over the Border in the mid 1600s. Legend has it every stone in the summit cairn, and also those at its feet, was carried by preacher Peden's congregation. King Coal and Ironstone mines also flourished above Bellingham from the 1700s to the turn of this century - note the old workings and spoil-heaps. Bellingham lies deep in sheep country, its annual show and sales exhibiting thousands of local Cheviots, Blackface and Greyface as well as "thae foreign breeds" such as Swaledales.

WALKS

In addition to treading the Pennine Way, either north or south, there is a delightful walk from Bellingham to Hareshaw Linn ("shaw" meaning wood and "linn" waterfall). It is a linear walk of 3 miles (4.8km) which crosses Hareshaw Burn by footbridge 12 times in total.

Beyond the Tourist Information Office in the main street a waymarked path follows Harshaw Burn north, soon to pass through two gates and by old mine workings on a good path before entering a delightful wooded dene. A mile (1.6km) and one small waterfall into this magic place, the thundering waters of Hareshaw Linn are heard before the sliding falls are seen. Take care underfoot as some rocks are slippery. The return journey is via the outward path.

12. FOX AND HOUNDS - Bellingham, Hexham, Northumberland NE48 2JP. (01434) 220478

There is little to suggest, save the words "Fox and Hounds" on the gable end, that this decaying "oyster" of a pub houses, according to one local paper, "Bellingham's best kept Secret". Disregard the uninviting exterior and examine the pearl inside, for this howff, known locally as "The Fox" or occasionally "The Nappers", has an undisputed pedigree. The weathered lintel says 1731, and the present landlady is a fourth-generation licensee.

The solitary bar-room, a great favourite with farmers and the local hunt, is the size of a farm kitchen, where "crack" and good cheer come by the glassful; aided and abetted by the Fox's 1/4 gill measures. A scattering of bar stools of assorted heights and wooden backed wall benches ease the legs, and a Bellingham chiming wall clock soothes the ears. Across the passage, in the parlour, a dumb piano pleases the eye, its playing days ended by a shower of strong ale. And all the while the unblinking gaze of North Tynedale's feathered inhabitants never falters, nor does the spirit of the welcome in this unique local.

OPEN:	May to September, 12 noon-3.30pm, 6.30-11pm October to April, 6.30-11pm Open all day on market days and show days
TYPE:	Free House
ON DRAUGHT:	Theakston Bitter, Stones Bitter, McEwan's Best Scotch, Harp Lager
BOTTLED:	Newcastle Brown Ale, Theakston Bitter, Guinness plus a selection of beers, stout, lager and cider
WHISKY:	Grouse and one malt. Spirit measures - 1/4 gill
WINE:	House white, medium
FOOD:	Bar snacks - crisps, nuts etc.

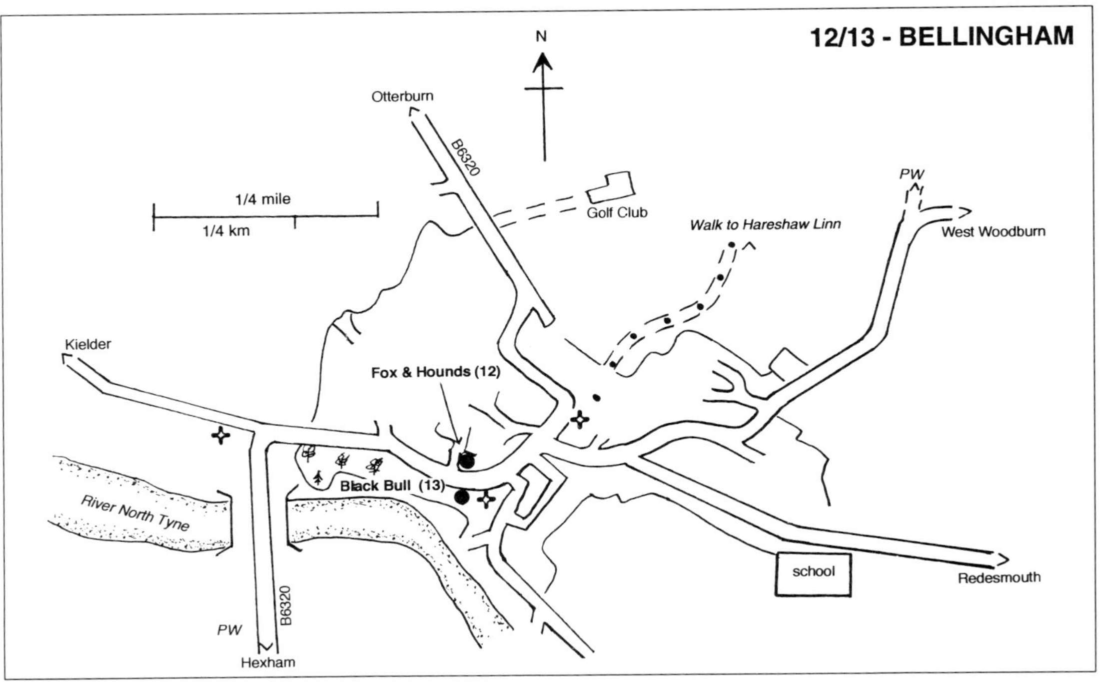
12/13 - BELLINGHAM
N
Otterburn
B6320
1/4 mile
1/4 km
Golf Club
PW
Walk to Hareshaw Linn
West Woodburn
Kielder
Fox & Hounds (12)
Black Bull (13)
River North Tyne
school
Redesmouth
B6320
PW
Hexham

ACCOMMODATION: No
FACILITIES: Darts, dominoes. No electronic devices
OPEN FIRES: Open gas fire, in a town with no gas pipes!
WALKERS: Most welcome, even with dirty boots and the "PW reek"
CHILDREN: In the small room
DOGS: Of course
PARKING: In the public car parks

ITEMS OF PUB INTEREST

The pub is often referred to, particularly by local farmers, as "The Nappers", in fond memory of a fell pony stallion called "Napper" who stood for many years in the stable yard of the "Fox".

The Border tradition of the $^{1}/_{4}$ gill spirit measure, coupled with the family name of the licensees, is immortalised by the pub's entry in the North Tyne raft race - "Potts' Quarter Measures".

The resident birds in the bar came into the possession of the present landlady's granny by default. A regular, having bought them in a local auction, deposited the cases in the Fox for collection later. He returned somewhat subdued and crestfallen for his wife refused to give the birds a perch and he was unable to re-sell; the birds patiently await collection.

Bellingham - Black Bull Hotel

13. BLACK BULL HOTEL - Bellingham, Hexham, Northumberland NE48 2JP. (01434) 220226

The white harled exterior of the Black Bull, a sentinel at the south end of the main street, is plain for all to see. A solid building as befits the area, originally a four square town house flanked by east and west wings of lower height. This gentleman's town house was converted in Victorian times to an inn.

A favourite with Pennine Wayfarers, the entrance porch leads directly from the street into a long low room housing the bar, lounge bar and games room. The unsympathetic hand of the brewer's shop fitters is in evidence; the heavy bar counter and accompanying pillars compensated by mirrored shelves of sparkling bottles and shining beer founts, the end wall adorned by a white-washed stone seated inglenook, large iron open stove and polished mantelshelf. Cushioned window seats, high bar stools coupled with a friendly pub atmosphere complete the beamed bar and lounge bar. At the far end is a spacious games room with a pool table. Kitchen improvements and a small room extention are in progress.

OPEN:	Monday to Saturday, 11am-11pm Sunday, 12 noon-3pm, 7-10.30pm
TYPE:	Free House
ON DRAUGHT:	Websters Yorkshire Bitter, Guinness, Carlsberg Lager, Foster's Lager, Symonds Scrumpy Jack Cider
BOTTLED:	Newcastle Brown Ale, Carslberg Special Brew, Holsten Pils, Budweiser and a selection of stout, lager, cider
WHISKY:	Proprietary blends, small selection of malts
WINE:	House, white, dry and medium; red
FOOD:	Bar and lounge bar, 12 noon-2pm, 7-9.30pm Menu includes daily specials
ACCOMMODATION:	2 doubles en-suite
FACILITIES:	Pool, darts, dominoes, bandit, video game
OPEN FIRES:	1 open stove in the bar
WALKERS:	Most welcome
CHILDREN:	Welcome
DOGS:	Allowed
PARKING:	Limited street-side and market place public parking

FOOD

A simple, satisfying menu prepared from local produce, the result of popular demand by locals and visitors, particularly Pennine Wayfarers who apparently develop a craving for the Bull's jumbo sausage and chips by the time they reach Bellingham.

GREENHAUGH

14. HOLLY BUSH INN - Greenhaugh, Tarset, Hexham, Northumberland NE48 1PW. (01434) 240391

Greenhaugh slumbers peacefully by an unclassified road, 4 miles (6.4km) north west of Bellingham, 8 miles (12.8km) south west from Otterburn and 5 miles (8km) east from Falstone and Kielder Water. The Holly Bush Inn stands on the west side of the road.

SITUATION *OS Map Landranger. Sheet 80 1:50,000 GR 795873*

Among the fine hamlets that shelter by the cleughs of Tynedale the solid stones of tranquil Greenhaugh sit well by Tarset Burn. Closeted by cottages, the Holly Bush Inn needs little or no ink from the pen to emphasise this is "a real old-fashioned country pub". There is nothing pseudo, fluorescent or chrome about this local, that basks in days gone by. Research revealed little else than proof of the inn's existence, and its landlord, James Potts in 1862, though no doubt it was an ale-house long before that. Today's bar originally doubled as the public bar, landlord's kitchen and eating quarters; since then a small back kitchen has been added and the small room beneath the stairs connected to the bar area. Little else has changed. Two low doors lead from the street, the low beamed, planked ceiling and linoed cement floor blending with two massive wall settles, one 12ft of pine wood flanking a 10ft pitch pine table. Various chairs of debatable age sit by the stone fireplace lulled by the restful "tick-tock" of a grandfather clock coyly recessed in the original wall. At the time of publication new licensees have taken over.

OPEN:	Monday to Saturday, 11am-3pm, 6.30-11pm Sunday, 12 noon-3pm, 7-10.30pm
TYPE:	Free House
ON DRAUGHT:	Newcastle Exhibition Ale, Tetley Bitter, Beamish Stout, LCL Pils (strong lager)
BOTTLED:	Newcastle Brown Ale, Theakston Bitter, Carlsberg Special Brew, plus a small selection of lagers and cider
WHISKY:	Proprietary blends and 1 malt
WINE:	Boxed white, dry and sweet
FOOD:	Only crisps, nuts and chocolates
ACCOMMODATION:	No
FACILITIES:	Darts and dominoes
OPEN FIRES:	1 in the bar
WALKERS:	Most welcome, including their dirty boots
CHILDREN:	Welcome, if only the law permitted

Greenhaugh - Holly Bush Inn

DOGS: Allowed
PARKING: On the street, please do not block access

ITEMS OF LOCAL INTEREST

The present stone fireplace in the Holly Bush was originally purchased from Harrods and installed into Greenhaugh Hall. Later it was removed and fitted in front of the old iron kitchen range, which still remains in situ. One mile south of Greenhaugh, just above the North Tyne, is Lanehead, where a now defunct inn called "The Drovers" stood, emphasising that this valley was a main drove route into England. Close by are the grassy mounds that once supported Tarset Castle, built in 1267 by John Comyn, a Scot and father of "Red Comyn" who was murdered in Greyfriars church, Dumfries, in 1306.

WALKS

A pleasant circular stroll of 2 miles (3.2km) from Greenhaugh alongside Tarset Burn. S from the village a signpost right indicates Boughthill and Greenhaugh Hall. Descend past the Hall to the ford crossing Tarset Burn (take care on the cement if wet). Do not cross but turn sharp right onto a narrow path between trees and fence to reach the low lying haughs. Follow the winding and picturesque Tarset N for 3/4 mile (1.2km) (rich in burnside wildlife) to reach two adjacent gates. Pass through both,

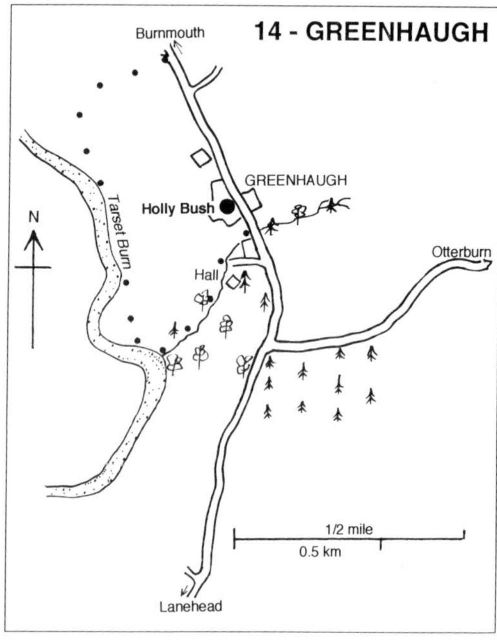

ascending the flat-topped knowe ahead (fine views) to turn the old school at Burbank on the N side. Follow the fence to a gate by the public road at a Y junction, where a signpost indicates "Greenhaugh 1/2 mile", for a pleasing return to the Holly Bush Inn.

FALSTONE

15. THE BLACKCOCK INN - Falstone, Hexham, Northumberland NE48 1AA. (01434) 240200 Colour photo opposite p33

The small village of Falstone is 10 miles (16km) west of Bellingham, 1/2 mile (0.8km) north of the Bellingham/Kielder road and 1 mile (1.6km) east from Kielder Water Dam. The Bellingham/Kielder lakeside road carries the classification C200.

SITUATION *OS Map Landranger. Sheet 80 1:50,000 GR 724875*

Falstone (from the Anglo Saxon fausten - stronghold) stands stone built and solid below the mass of Kielder Water reservoir. Positioned between two churches the Blackcock carries on its tradition of "shelter and sustenance". In the early 1600s this simple farmhouse brewed its own beer, a practice that was ended by a band of marauding Scots. The farmhouse ruins were refashioned as

Falstone - The Blackcock Inn

a single-storey thatched ale-house, and so they remained until the late 1800s. Today, this cheerful, popular pub has much to offer: a bar that still retains its farmhouse kitchen feel with a "black leaded range" set in the bare stone wall, "clippie mat" on the tiled floor (no problem for walkers), cushioned settles and a stuffed blackcock. The lounge bar, doubling up as a pool room, separated by the staircase is equally pleasant; fading photographs, cigarette card collections, plated cats and china cats, milk-churns and a cast-iron stove all shout "welcome". A small dining room with a marble fireplace, a non-smoking residents' lounge and en-suite bedrooms complete this "canny wee pub".

OPEN:	11am-3pm, 6.30-11pm (Sunday, 7-10.30pm) 11am-11pm for a Saturday function
TYPE:	Free House
ON DRAUGHT:	Always 4 real ales, eg. Devil's Water, Vaux Extra Special, Longstone Bitter, Castle Eden Ale. Theakston Best Bitter, Whitbread's Best Scotch, Trophy Bitter, Murphy's Irish Stout, Heineken Lager, LCL Pils, Symonds' Scrumpy Jack
BOTTLED:	Newcastle Brown Ale, Wee Heavy, Sweet Stouts, Carlsberg Special plus lagers and ciders
WHISKY:	Proprietary blends and selected malts
WINE:	House, white dry and medium. Wine list selection of 13
FOOD:	12 noon-2pm and evening, bar, lounge bar and dining room
ACCOMMODATION:	2 double, 1 single bedroom en-suite, 1 twin and 1 single
FACILITIES:	Stair lift to bedrooms and lounge, picnic benches on lawn. Darts, dominoes, draughts, pool. Local music
OPEN FIRES:	Bar, lounge bar and dining room
WALKERS:	Most welcome
CHILDREN:	Welcome, except in bar
DOGS:	Welcome, two resident Jack Russells
PARKING:	Limited number at the pub entrance

FOOD

A selection of mouth-watering home made pies and giant-sized yorkshire puds, filled with the inn's special recipes. À la carte also available in the dining room. Quantity and quality to satisfy The Alternative Pennine Wayfarer and all dished up by genial staff.

ITEMS OF LOCAL INTEREST

This wild and windswept land has, since 1926, succumbed to a cloak of conifers and endless acres of water. The initial pain has through time subsided and what is visible today is now acceptable. Kielder Water, the

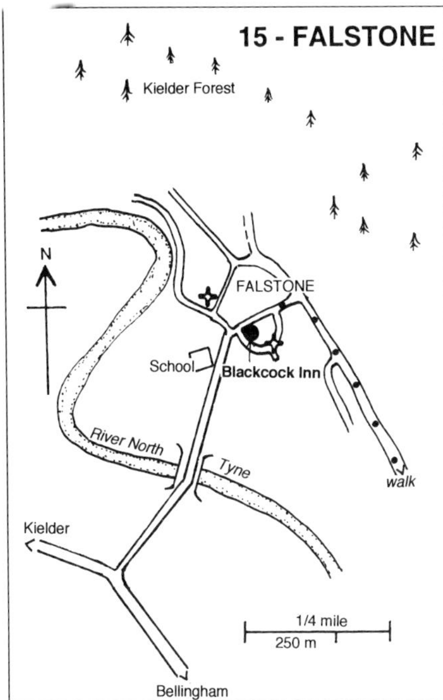

largest reservoir in Britain, fills the North Tyne valley with 45,000 million gallons of water covering 2,800 acres, restrained by a dam 170ft high and 3,750ft long. Encircling it all is Kielder Forest, Borders Forest Park, 30 miles by 27 miles, the largest man-made forest in Europe, yielding 1,000 tons plus of useable timber per day.

WALKS

For a fell and riverside walk leave Falstone via the old rail bridge, SE and E on Donkleywood lane; after 1$^{1/2}$ miles (2.4km) turn left onto a signposted track ascending NE to Slaty Ford. At this picturesque ford swing S with the waymarked path winding with the dene to Old Hall, beyond the old railway line. At Donkleywood road turn right for $^{1/2}$ mile to the "Public Path" signpost. A stiled and waymarked path fringes the North Tyne then returns to the lane at Donkleywood, returning W to Falstone for a Blackcock "Yorkie Pud".

Forest Enterprise and Northumbrian Water Authority have in recent years encouraged outdoor interests, waymarking a selection of fine walks.

STANNERSBURN

16. THE PHEASANT INN - Stannersburn, Falstone, Hexham, Northumberland NE48 1DD. (01434) 240382

$^{1/2}$ mile (0.8km) south of Falstone and 1 mile (1.6km) east of Kielder

Stannersburn - The Pheasant Inn

Water dam; on the unclassified road between Bellingham 10 miles (16km) south, and Kielder village 10 miles (16km) north.

SITUATION *OS Map Landranger. Sheet 80 1:50,000 GR 722867*
A traditional Northumbrian border inn that has endured a chequered past from the 1630s to 1975; a farm ale-house, and a tax and mail centre called The Crown, but known locally as "Stanners". It was then refurbished and renamed The Pheasant. Bared stone walls, low beamed ceilings and the friendly staff give character to the inn and a comforting welcome to those who journey through the North Tyne valley. Two bars, public left and lounge right, decorated with stuffed pheasants (naturally), agricultural artifacts (a working saddle of a railway packhorse) and sepia photographs of days goneby. Both bars, lined with wooden-backed cushioned settles and ample tables have connecting, highly polished counters and shining brass that shout welcome to all.

A stone archway from the lounge bar leads into the beamed and red carpeted dining room, warmly furnished with fine pine tables and chairs. The spacious games room, its walls lined with seats, adjoins the public bar.

OPEN:	Monday to Saturday, 11am-3pm, 6-11pm
	Sunday 12 noon-3pm, 7-10.30pm
TYPE:	Free House
ON DRAUGHT:	Theakston XB, Theakston Best Bitter, Newcastle Exhibition, McEwan's

	Best Scotch, Guinness, Harp Lager, Strongbow Cider
BOTTLED/CANS:	Newcastle Brown Ale, Budweiser, Carlsberg Special Brew, Holsten Pils, McEwan's Low Alcohol
WHISKY:	Proprietary blends, plus a selection of malts
WINE:	House wines, dry/medium chilled white, red. Elderflower cordial, barrelled sherry, selective wine list
FOOD:	Mid-day 12-2.15pm and evening bar/lounge bar, overflow in pool room. No smoking dining room, evening à la carte
ACCOMMODATION:	8 bedrooms, twin/double with en-suite facilites; converted from an adjacent barn and hemmel
FACILITIES:	Garden-trestle tables. Games room with pool table, darts, dominoes, draughts
OPEN FIRES:	In winter in the bar and the lounge bar
WALKERS:	Welcome
CHILDREN:	Welcome, in the games room or if eating
DOGS:	No
PARKING:	Car park, walkers' cars may be left with management approval

FOOD

Freshly prepared and cooked local produce providing traditional Sunday roasts attract visitors from far and wide. The bar blackboards of 19 choice snacks and dishes, such as steak and kidney pie and well cooked fresh vegetables, confirm the various food awards.

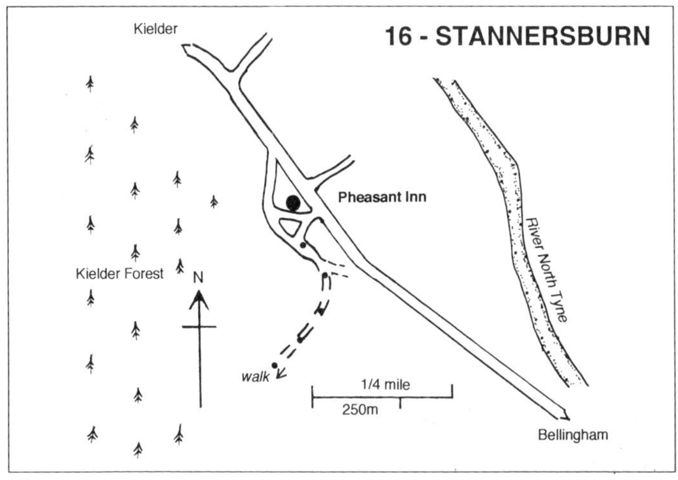

ITEMS OF LOCAL INTEREST

One mile from Kielder Water reservoir and surrounded by Kielder Forest, the inn offers a base for cruising, sailing, water ski-ing, wind-surfing, fishing, long or short walks and pony trekking. Nearby Kielder Castle Visitors' Centre provides a wealth of information about the area.

A simple remembrance cross, 1939-45, erected near the burn and the inn's car park by Luftwaffe air crew, remembers comrades who perished nearby.

WALKS

Short waymarked walks by Kielder Water and Kielder Forest can be enjoyed - route details from the respective information centres.

A longer walk, S from the Pheasant, opens up extensive views of the North Tyne valley. Behind the pub a forest road, waymarked APW, ascends S fringing the trees. As the road descends take the first left, winding down to Smales Burn bridge. Leave the road and follow the burn S for 100yds or so to the delightful water cascade of Smales Leap (an ideal picnic spot).

Return to the bridge, cross the road and with the quarry on the right make for the rocky outcrop above the burn (keep a sharp eye open for adders). A narrow grassy trod, between conifers and the burn, winds N to a wicket gate, waymarked APW. Continue N over open, in places damp, country to the forest fringes and the waymarked outward track from Stannersburn.

Chapter 2
Scottish Borders - East

BURNMOUTH

17. THE FLEMINGTON INN - Burnmouth, Berwickshire TD14 5SL. (01890) 781277

Burnmouth, a fishing hamlet of character, clings tightly to the Berwickshire cliffs as the A1(T) rushes by. 6 miles (9.6km) north of Berwick and 2½ miles (4km) south of Eyemouth via the A1107. The Flemington Inn sits well in the elbow of both roads.

SITUATION *OS Map Landranger. Sheet 67 1:50,000 GR 953609*

Listed as "The First and Last in Scotland", this white walled, red shuttered gem of a pub started life as two cottages, and has, due to its unique position, catered for both local fishermen and travellers on the busy Edinburgh to Newcastle route, for centuries. Step inside this tiny, friendly, family run pub and it

Burnmouth - The Flemington Inn

appears to expand on entry, its single bar counter, with shining taps and bottles, serving both the bar on the right and the lounge bar to the left. Space is well managed, the dartboard being "boxed-in" to prevent flying arrows. Buttoned wall seats and a scattering of solid tables provide comfort for tired limbs. Local scenes by local artists (Burnmouth is a magnet), sepia fishing photos, jugs and well tended greenery all add a smile to the two bright rooms with the tiny windows. Have your walk first, then relax.

OPEN:	Monday to Friday, 11am-12 midnight Saturday, 11am-11.30pm Sunday, 12.30-11.30pm In winter closed 2.30-5pm
TYPE:	Free House
ON DRAUGHT:	Burton Ale, Boddingtons Bitter, Dryboroughs Heavy, Alloa Export, Guinness, Lowenbrau Strong Lager, Skol Lager, Gaymer's Old English Cider
BOTTLED:	Newcastle Brown Ale, Carlsberg Special Brew plus a selection of beers, stout, lager and cider
WHISKY:	Proprietary blends and 20 thoughtful malts

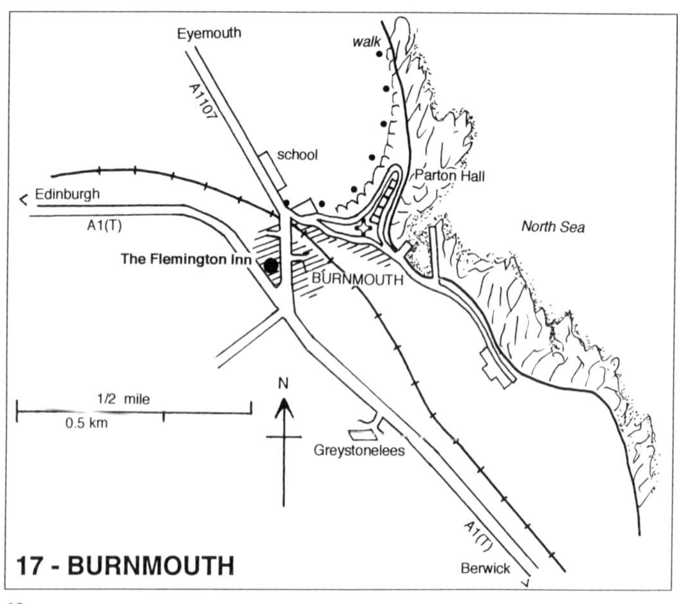

WINE:	House white, dry-medium-sweet; red. Listed on small wine list and blackboard
FOOD:	Bar lunches 12.30-2.30pm (Sunday 2pm). Evening meals 6.30-9pm. Les Routiers and Pub Taste of Scotland
ACCOMMODATION:	No
FACILITIES:	Quiz nights, darts, dominoes, bandit, subdued music. Tables on the small lawn in summer
OPEN FIRES:	Look alike gas fires in the bar and lounge bar
WALKERS:	Most welcome, as are divers, cyclists, geologists etc.
CHILDREN:	In the lounge bar if eating, up to 8pm
DOGS:	Bar only under control
PARKING:	Private and public parking at the front

FOOD

Sea food, naturally, is a favourite and is presented with flair and imagination - try the smoked salmon omelette or fisherman's platter; also popular is the steak pie or pheasant in cider and apple. Home-cooked with local products when possible, the Flemington serves quality pub grub without the pretentious misnomer "restaurant". Menus and blackboards display the "goodies"; for parties or weekends please book.

ITEMS OF LOCAL INTEREST

Flemington, a name given to two local farms and the inn, is derived from a centuries old connection with Flemish merchants who anchored their ships in Eyemouth harbour and grazed their flocks on the green hillsides. Other visitors also came by sea; smugglers with brandy and claret rowed in by stealth to conceal the duty-free in the nearby old houses of Fairneyside, Greystonelees and Catch-a-Penny.

WALKS

An invigorating 3 mile (4.8km) cliff-top geological and wildlife journey, N from Burnmouth to Eyemouth. Take the gate by the school, N from the railway bridge, behind the houses onto the cliffs high above Partanhall. Continue N with the guiding wall/fence, on a narrow path which switches sides and in places is exposed *(careful)*, past Breeches Rock to the phenomena of the 338ft (103m) cliffs of Fancove Head. Marvel at the rock formations and S the distant Northumberland coastline. Continue with wall/fence descending via Horse Head and Scout Point to lower cliffs, and finally left via the golf course then football pitches to the screeching gulls and swaying masts of Eyemouth harbour.

EYEMOUTH

18. SHIP HOTEL - Harbour Road, Eyemouth, Berwickshire TD14 5HT (01890) 750224 ***Colour photo opposite p64***

Eyemouth, a major fishing port on the rocky coast of Berwickshire; 50 miles (80km) south east of Edinburgh and 8½ miles (13.6km) north-west of Berwick-upon-Tweed via the A1107. The Ship Hotel is situated on the harbour front.

SITUATION *OS Map Landranger. Sheet 67 1:50,000 GR 946643*

The long harbour of Eyemouth, its entrance ringed by the dark jaws of Hurker rocks, its walls flanked by a phalanx of huddled buildings, is a visual delight when packed tight with resting boats and screaming gulls.

Barely a road's width away from the harbour stands the white rough-cast Ship Hotel. An ale house/"rum shop" since the late 1700s, it has always serviced the needs of Eyemouth's fishing community. A spacious bar room with barrel stools, iron/wood tables, padded wall seats, lino and carpeted floor, old salts photos, fishing memorabilia and cosy open fire confirms this is a fisherman's local. The adjacent lounge bar, once a cobbler's workshop, is equally marine, its walls displaying some delightful seascapes. The carpet and the comfort, however, suggest it's not the place for dripping dirty boots.

OPEN:	All year, 11am-12 midnight
TYPE:	Tied House, Alloa Brewery
ON DRAUGHT:	Two changing guest ales, eg Caledonian Brewery 70/-, Orkney Dark Raven, Tetley Best Bitter, Dryborough's Heavy, Alloa Special 70/- & Light Ale, Guinness, Carslberg & Skol Lager, Lowenbrau, Gaymer's Cider
BOTTLED:	Newcastle Brown Ale, blackboard listed lagers, plus a selection of beers, stout and cider
WHISKY:	Proprietary blends and 20 selected malts
RUM:	Selection of 40
WINE:	House wines,white, dry and medium: red. Careful wine list
FOOD:	Bar and lounge bar, 12 noon-2.30pm and 6-10pm. Menu plus 3 daily specials on the blackboard
ACCOMMODATION:	5 double/twin rooms, all en-suite
FACILITIES:	Darts, dominoes, bandit, quiz machine, league quiz nights. Beer "garden" overlooking harbour, drying room, sea-shanties by "the Podlies"
OPEN FIRES:	Coal, in bar

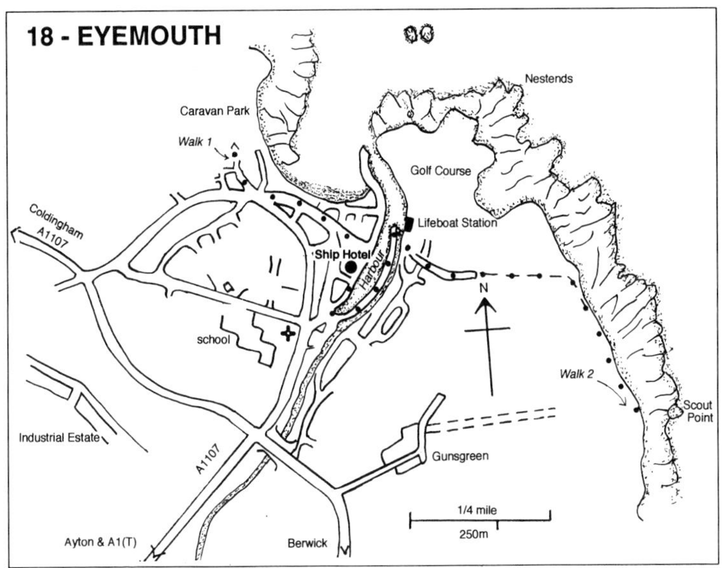

WALKERS:	Welcome
CHILDREN:	Welcome, children's licence
DOGS:	In bar only
PARKING:	At the rear, can be left by arrangement

FOOD

With local produce such as fresh fish and border meats cooked on the premises, the daily changed specials are very popular with regulars and summer visitors.

ITEMS OF LOCAL INTEREST

Eyemouth, the most southerly seaport in Scotland, was mentioned in a twelfth-century charter granted to Coldinghame Priory, and in 1597 became a free port. Later it was to become the Border's smuggling centre - "dark and cunning of aspect". The sea for centuries has been life, and on occasions death, to Eyemouth; as in the great storm of 1881 when 189 fishermen were lost, including 129 men from Eyemouth.

Robert Burns arrived in May 1787, "Saturday - Come up a bold shore, and over a wild country, to Eyemouth, sup and sleep at Mrs Grieve's". The colourful Herring Queen Festival is held every July.

WALKS

A spectacular coastal and cliff walk of 4 miles (6.4km), from Eyemouth harbour NW via Coldingham Bay to St Abbs. Go from the caravan park by Hairy Ness to the rocks of Callercove Point, where a distinct path turns inland with the wall before descending by Abbey Burn (note the many wild flowers) to the shore. Follow the shoreline and the low cliffs to Coldingham Bay, a crescent of golden sand. Steps ascend N onto a walkway, 3/4 mile (1.2km) to the picturesque fishing village of St Abbs.

Details of further varied walks from Eyemouth and district can be obtained from the TIC.

PAXTON

19. HOOLIT'S NEST - Paxton, Berwickshire TD15 1TE. (01289) 386267

The village of Paxton nestling between Whiteadder Water and Tweed, a mere 3/4 mile (1.2km) into Scotland, is not easy to find. 6 miles (9.6km) west of Berwick-upon-Tweed on the B6461 two minor signposted roads lead north for 1/2 mile to the village.

SITUATION *OS Map Landranger. Sheet 74 1:50,000 GR 935531*

The Hoolit's Nest in the centre of Paxton looks inviting. Built in the early 1880s close by the mercat cross (now sadly demolished) it was, not surprisingly, called "The Cross"; later known locally as "Paxton Pub", but now renamed the Hoolit's Nest. Replica owls, in excess of 200, now nest or perch in every conceivable place. Of the five native owls only the long eared owl is not represented, an omission that hopefully will be remedied.

The entrance porch steps directly into the shiny warm welcome of the L-shaped public bar, its stone counter crowned with polished wood and glistening hand pumps. Leatherette buttoned wall seats and small tables make the most of the limited space. The carpeted and curtained dining room, left on entering, is divided by a stone arch. Bright and cheerful, its converted iron treadle sewing machine tables, a fishing map and game flies join the ubiquitous owls on the open stone walls.

OPEN: Monday-Saturday, 11am-2.30pm, 6.30-11pm
Sunday, 12.30-2.30pm, 6.30-11pm

TYPE: Free House

ON DRAUGHT: Merlin's Ale, Caledonian 80/-, plus 1 guest real ale, Dryboroughs Heavy, Guinness, Carlsberg Lager, Symonds' Scrumpy Jack

BOTTLED: Newcastle Brown Ale, Wee Heavy, Carlsberg Special Brew, selection

Eyemouth - Ship Hotel
Morebattle - Templehall Inn

Ancrum - Cross Keys Inn
Melrose - Burts Hotel

	of stout, lager and cider
WHISKY:	Proprietary blends, plus a small group of selected malts
WINE:	House white, dry/sweet, red. Varied wine list of 15
FOOD:	Bar lunch 12 noon-2pm, dining room 7-9pm. No food on Mondays. Menu together with daily specials blackboard
ACCOMMODATION:	No
FACILITIES:	Disabled persons' ramp in entrance, dining room and toilets. Patio with two tables. Bar games - darts, draughts, dominoes and cards
OPEN FIRES:	Gas look-alike in bar
WALKERS:	Welcome, please leave muddy gear in the entrance porch
CHILDREN:	Welcome in the dining room, up to 8.30pm
DOGS:	No
PARKING:	Car park at the east end, cars left with owner's consent

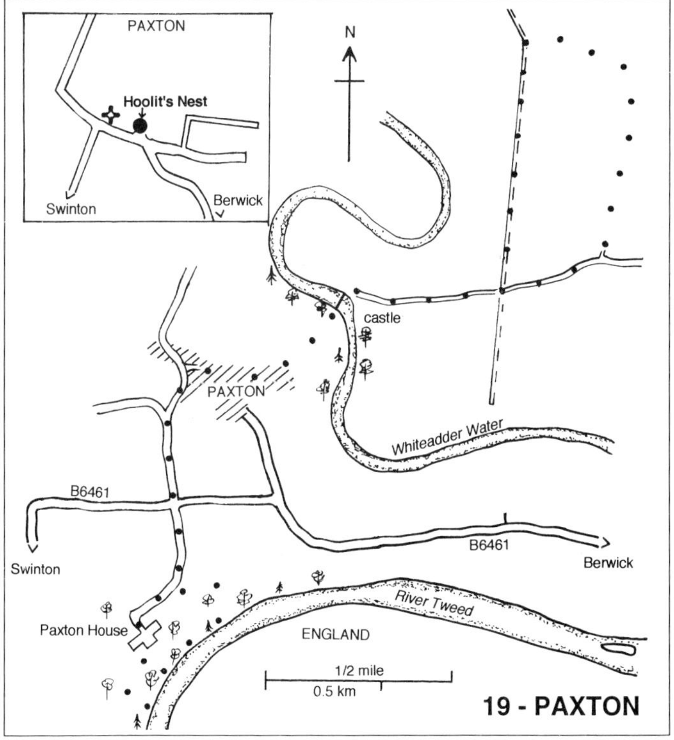

Paxton - Hoolit's Nest

FOOD

Freshly made sandwiches to the three course Special Sunday Spread are displayed on a blackboard, served in helpings that will satisfy most appetites. The evening menu is extensive, but not beyond the range of the chef. Vegetarian and children's choice.

ITEMS OF LOCAL INTEREST

Paxton House, built in 1758 by the Laird of Wedderburn for his intended bride, the daughter of Frederick the Great of Prussia, stands in 70 acres between the village and the Tweed. Open to the public.

Above the nearby Whiteadder Water stand the ruins of the stronghold of Edrington, upstream the fifteenth-century keep of Hutton Castle. The old toll-bar at Paxton marks the boundary of "The Liberties of Berwick".

Hutton for auld wives,
Broadmeadows for swine:
Paxton for drunken wives,
And salmon sae fine;

WALKS

1) Left (E) out of the pub, for a $3^{1/2}$ miles (5.6km) walk. Left at the council houses, then right to a hedge-side path N, descending to a footbridge

spanning the picturesque water of Whiteadder. Beyond a derelict corn mill ascend right with the lane continuing E to cross the Border into England, with fine views of Berwick and the coastline to Holy Island. Turn left by an electrical sub-station to High Cocklaw, left again for 3/4 mile (1.2km) on the Border Line to join the outward route from Paxton. 2) From the Hoolit's Nest, W through the village taking 1st left for 1/2 mile (0.8km), to the Lion Gates at Paxton House. Halfway down the drive turn right onto a woodland path leading to the house (a visit is most rewarding). From the house a circular pathway winds down to and alongside the Tweed returning to the main drive. Return to Paxton.

ALLANTON

20. THE ALLANTON INN - Allanton by Duns, Berwickshire TD11 3JZ. (01890) 818260 *Photo p2*

Allanton, a small Berwickshire village, lines the B6347 above the junction of Whiteadder and Blackadder Waters; 1 1/2 miles (2.4km) south of Chirnside and 10 1/2 miles (16.8km) north of Coldstream. Allanton Inn is centrally placed, east side of the main street.

SITUATION *OS Map Landranger. Sheet 74 1:50,000 GR 866543*

Starting life in 1835 as a pub serving the thriving agricultural community (note the tethering rings), it acquired coaching inn status and the name Red Lion in 1840. Of local stone the inn has grown over the years, the dining room from a grocer's shop, the gent's loo from the original bar and the lounge bar from the old kitchen. Thoughtful planning and a new name in 1981 have produced today's inn. Entry into the spacious L-shaped carpeted bar and lounge bar is accompanied by the squeaky rhythm of the swinging inn sign, work of a local artist. A fringe of flagstones surround the pine bar counter and a good balance of cushioned wall seats and tables cater for the choice of "sit or stand"; with the red-brick fireplace the winter focal point in this friendly local. A small dining room opens from the bar, its walls decorated with dried flowers that distract the eye from today's wooden beams. A much used functions room and bedrooms occupy the upper floor.

OPEN:	Monday to Friday, 12 noon-2.30pm, 6-11pm Saturday to Sunday, 12 noon-11.30pm (Sunday open 12.30pm)
TYPE:	Free House
ON DRAUGHT:	Belhaven 80/-, Adnams Extra, Courage Directors, Broughton Merlin, Belhaven 70/-, Belhaven St Andrews, Belhaven Best, Murphy's Stout, Tennant's Lager, In summer, a still cider

BOTTLED:	Newcastle Brown Ale, Carlsberg Special Brew, plus a selection of stout, lager and cider
WHISKY:	Proprietary blends with 8-12 selected malts
WINE:	House white, dry and medium; red. Small wine list with wine of the month on the bar blackboard
FOOD:	Served during bar opening hours. Menu plus daily specials on bar blackboard
ACCOMMODATION:	2 doubles, 1 twin, 1 single - shared facilities
FACILITIES:	Darts, dominoes, cards, bandit, TV; regular live music nights. Trestle tables in the garden
OPEN FIRES:	In the bar and the functions room
WALKERS:	Welcome, with all outdoor enthusiasts
CHILDREN:	Welcome, children's licence
DOGS:	Welcome, not in dining room
PARKING:	At the front, on the roadside apron

FOOD SPECIALS

Innovative dishes of in-season local produce, home cooked with thought and flair, eg. game week, using local pheasant, pigeon and hare. Soups are thoroughly recommended. Vegetarian dishes available.

ITEMS OF LOCAL INTEREST

Nearby Allanbank, haunt of one of Scotland's most famous apparitions, "Pearlin Jeanne", operated in the 1800s one of the first hydro-electric schemes, providing power for the house and water for Allanton. Above

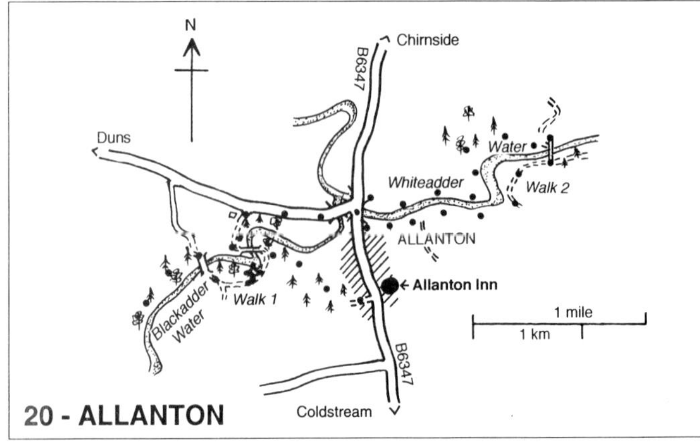

Blackadder Water teeters the defunct stronghold of Edmund Blackadder circa 1500s, the source for the TV series of that ilk.

Jim Clark, Berwickshire's world champion racing driver, had connections with Allanton and the inn, as had novelist Anne Dickinson, née Semple.

WALKS

1) A pleasing walk of 3½ miles (5.6km) via the haunting ruins of Blackadder House. From the Inn pass by the old lodge gates, continue W through scrub to a crumbling bridge, an old quarry and the remains of Blackadder Castle. Continue S and W skirting the trees before descending a farm road to a second bridge. Turn left for a stroll in the old gardens of Blackadder. Return to the quarry, cross the Blackadder ascending N via Tofthill; turn E to return to Allanton.

2) A riverside walk of 2½ miles (4km) on both sides of Whiteadder Water from Whiteadder bridge (by R Stevenson). Follow the N bank for 1 mile (1.6km) to the cliffs and woods of Whitehall, winding N to Blue Stone footbridge. Cross to the south bank and walk W with the river, returning to Allanton.

SWINTON

21. WHEATSHEAF - Main Street, Swinton, Berwickshire TD11 3JJ. (01890) 860257

Swinton, a typical Berwickshire village straddles the junction of the A6112 Duns to Coldstream and the B6461 Berwick to Kelso roads. The roadside Wheatsheaf Inn stands north of the village green.

SITUATION *OS Map Landranger. Sheet 74 1:50,000 GR 834474*

The Wheatsheaf's conservatory windows and red sandstone frontage overlook the most unusual village green in the Borders. The football pitch's centre spot is crowned by a weathered nineteenth-century stone cross, built to record the last boar killed in the area. Positioned in the heart of the wheat-growing Merse, the Wheatsheaf has retained its original name and in recent years has deservedly grown in popularity.

The bar is small and cosy, its walls lined with cushioned wooden settles and tables by a warming open fire. The lounge, with its low ceilinged bar tucked around the corner, sports a log-burning stone fireplace, a long oak settle, cushioned window seats and wheel backed chairs observed by agricultural prints, a stuffed partridge, pheasant and Weatsheaf motifs. The recently opened "no smoking" sun lounge is light, bright and airy, consisting of pine beams, dressed stone walls and much glass. A small intimate dining room completes the scenario.

The inn can get very busy; a simple 'phone call can save disappointment.

OPEN:	Tuesday to Saturday, 11am-2.30pm, 6-11pm Sunday, 12.30-2.30pm, 6.30-11pm
TYPE:	Free House
ON DRAUGHT:	Wheatsheaf Ale, Greenmantle Ale, Broughton Special Bitter, Carlsberg Lager, Warsteiner Bier, Dry Blackthorn Cider
BOTTLED:	Selection of beers, stout, lager and cider
WHISKY:	Standard proprietary blends plus 12 selected malts
WINE:	House wines, Australian dry/German medium white; French/Australian red. Plus a wine list of width and quality
FOOD:	Lunch-time/evening during opening hours. Meals in the bar only as overflow. Menus and daily specials blackboards
ACCOMMODATION:	2 double (1 en-suite with shower), 2 twin
FACILITIES:	Beer garden. In bar dominoes, darts, bandit and pool. Walking guides for sale
OPEN FIRES:	Lounge bar and bar
WALKERS:	Welcome; if in boots bar only please
CHILDREN:	Children's licence if eating to 8pm, but not in bar
DOGS:	Sorry, no dogs
PARKING:	Street-side and in front of the beer garden

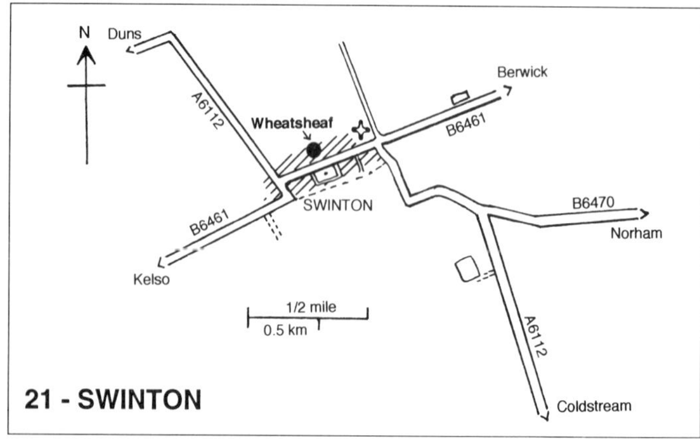

Swinton - Wheatsheaf

FOOD

Waitress served, local home cooked food at all tables (seats 60). A menu of 8 starters, 10 main course and 7 sweets, plus a blackboard of daily specials, ranging from local smoked salmon to two medallions of Scotch beef on a rich claret sauce laced with a julienne of wild mushrooms. Dishes that will please the most voracious walkers.

ITEMS OF LOCAL INTEREST

Swinton's querky pitch, with the stone centre spot, was used for matches between locals and itinerant Irish labourers. With pre-match refreshments liberally taken in the Wheatsheaf, small wonder the visiting team ran into the "twelfth man", to remain well and truly tackled.

The Swintons of that Ilk are among the most ancient families in Scotland. Authentic documents record them at Swinton in AD1060, Edulf de Swinton receiving the property from Malcolm Carnmore.

WALKS

Ringed by well tended arable land, of an open and flat character, there is little or no scope save that of the country lane, to ease away the excesses of the Wheatsheaf. A short signposted pathway runs the length of the village, on the south side, between the fields and the houses. Another signposted pathway, a yard or so W of the west end, runs S for two fields then peters out! The view of Cheviot to the south is the only item of interest. For walks of character I suggest a visit to the coastal cliffs of Berwickshire or the nearby Lammermuir Hills.

KIRK YETHOLM

22. BORDER HOTEL - The Green, Kirk Yetholm, Roxburghshire TD5 8PQ. (01573) 420237

Kirk Yetholm, omega of the Pennine Way, nestles beneath the north eastern Cheviots; close to the B6352 and the B6401, 8 miles (12.8km) south-east of Kelso and 15 miles (24km) west of Wooler. The Border Hotel stands on the north side of the village green.

SITUATION *OS Map Landranger. Sheet 74 1:50,000 GR 828283*

A village inn known as "The Nags" Head stood on this site from the seventeenth century, today's thatched section being the original pub. A hatch by the door of this section marks an act of discrimination practised against Yetholm Gypsies years ago; as entry into the inn was forbidden their ale was poured out through the small hatch (today's letter box).

Today's bar, open to all, is entered via a porch displaying a specials blackboard and a heartfelt appeal to walkers. The black-beamed bar, nicotine stained by generations of gasping Pennine Wayfarers, is no doubt a welcome haven. Buttoned wall seats, a sprinkling of tables, a black floor, agricultural "bits" and pieces, and a variety of prints (including A.Wainwright) are all secondary to the inviting polished wood counter with the shining pumps. The long lounge is carpeted and well lit, with french windows leading to a paved and grassed beer garden. A resident's lounge and four bedrooms complete the scenario.

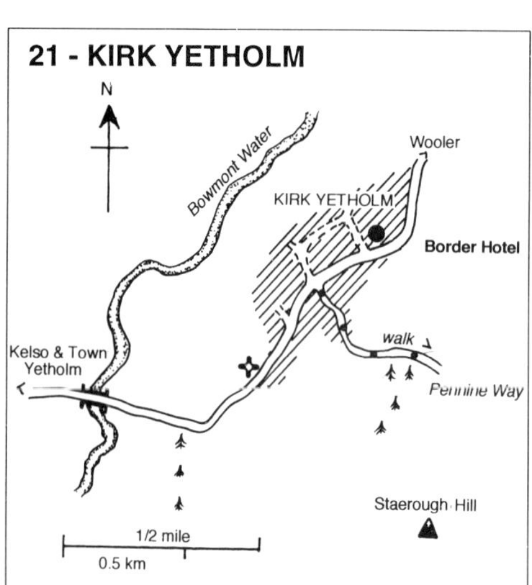

OPEN:	Summer (May to October),	11am-11pm (w/e 12 midnight)
	Winter (November to April),	12 noon-2.30pm, 6.30-11pm
TYPE:	Free House	
ON DRAUGHT:	Winter 1 guest ale, summer indigenous ales. Caledonian 80/-, Greenmantle Ale, Aitken's Ale, Tennent's 80/- & Special 70/-, Tennent's Lager, Guinness	
BOTTLED:	Newcastle Brown Ale, Carlsberg Special Brew plus a selection of beers, stout, lager and cider	
WHISKY:	Proprietary blends and a goodly range of malts	
WINE:	House white, medium; red; European wine list	
FOOD:	Served in the bar and the lounge, 12 noon-2pm, 6-9pm. Specials blackboard and menu	
ACCOMMODATION:	2 double, 2 twin, 2 toilets, bath/shower	
FACILITIES:	Beer garden, pool room, darts on match nights only. Background local radio	
OPEN FIRES:	All purpose burner in bar	
WALKERS:	Welcome, both need each other	
CHILDREN:	In the lounge and pool room only	
DOGS:	In the bar only	
PARKING:	Limited to the inn front, otherwise around the green	

Kirk Yetholm - Border Hotel

FOOD

Local butchers supply Border meat for the generous helpings, much appreciated by Pennine Wayfarers.

ITEMS OF LOCAL INTEREST

The Cherrytrees road to Yetholm, with wondrous views of the Cheviots, passes Thirlstane, one time home to Dr Scott, Charles II's physician, who, because of his skill as a chemist, was to the good folk of Yetholm a wizard; one room in the house is still referred to as 'Warlock's Room'.

Kirk Yetholm, as opposed to Town Yetholm, is perhaps best remembered as home to the largest colony of gypsies in Scotland; one of them, "King" Will Faa, was the proud father of 24.

WALKS

Conveniently placed at the foothills of the Cheviots, Kirk Yetholm has easy and immediate access to many fine and varied walks.

Try a quick dash up the rocky flanks of Stearough Hill, for immediate views of Kirk and Town Yetholm, the Bowmont Valley and the surrounding hills. For a longer, but even finer grandstand utilise the Pennine Way to Halter Burn, via Stob Stone (on passing, line-up the Eildons) and White Law. Descend to the ruins of Old Halterburn on the valley floor using the picturesque escape route of the Pennine Way, via Halter Burn, to return to Kirk Yetholm. For longer walks of challenge and character see *The Border Country* by Alan Hall, Chapter 1, Walks 5-10.

DUNS

23. WHIP AND SADDLE - Market Square, Duns, Berwickshire TD11 3SQ. (01361) 883215

Duns, an ancient Scottish burgh, sits easily between the southern Lammermuir Hills and the stiff acres of the Merse; 15 miles (24km) west of Berwick-upon-Tweed on the A6105 and A6112. The Whip and Saddle is on the north-east side of the Market Square.

SITUATION *OS Map Landranger. Sheet 74 1:50,000 GR 785539*

Brunton, the original town of Duns stood on Duns Law, cruelly sacked in 1545 by Hertford, Henry VIII's grim-reaper. A new settlement was founded on the present site in 1588 and made a Burgh of Barony in 1670. Records of a coaching inn by the site of the Whip and Saddle go back to 1798. The present pub,

Duns - Whip and Saddle

adjoining the sleeping quarters of the first inn, has had many names, including "Grey Horse Hotel" and "Royal Hotel/Bar".

The entire ground floor consists of a pleasant Bar, run by a landlord whose concern for his customers is evident. Surrounded by an original 3ft thick wall with recessed stained-glass windows, the floor is planked with Oregon pine, the bar counter topped by fine Canadian oak and the nicotine cured ceiling shines bright with varnish. Thoughtfully illuminated prints and old photographs grace the walls, where two curved booths with buttoned chesterfields, divided by patterned glass, add leisurely comfort. Include the coat hooks, drinks shelves and hidden TV and it all adds up to a friendly relaxing local with well kept ale. Up the stair a convenient family room and a spotless kitchen.

OPEN:	Every day, 11am-11pm Friday closes 12 midnight, Saturday closes 11.30pm
TYPE:	Free House
ON DRAUGHT:	Guest ales on the blackboard. Morland Speckled Hen, Deuchars IPA, Theakston XB and BB, McEwan's 70/- & 60/-, Guinness, McEwan's Lager, Blackthorn Cider
BOTTLED:	Newcastle Brown Ale, Becks Bier, Budweiser, plus a selection of beers, stout, lager and cider
WHISKY:	Proprietary blends and 3 popular malts
WINE:	4 house wines, white dry, medium, sweet; red
FOOD:	Lunch 12 noon-2pm, evening parties by arrangement. Filled rolls and sandwiches available all day

ACCOMMODATION: No
FACILITIES: "Shut the Box" - a medieval dice game, darts, dominoes
OPEN FIRES: No
WALKERS: Welcome
CHILDREN: Welcome in the family room
DOGS: Guide dogs only
PARKING: In the adjacent town square

FOOD

Home cooked using fresh local produce when available, no frozen fish or meat. A small but popular menu with daily specials on a blackboard, a firm favourite with regulars is the home prepared "beery battered" fresh haddock or cod. Vegetarians and children well catered for.

ITEMS OF LOCAL INTEREST

Birthplace in 1265 of John Duns Scotus, Franciscan, Oxford professor of Theology, defender of the Immaculate Conception, gaining the contemptuous nickname "Dr Subtilis". His tomb in Cologne states "SCOTIA ME GENUIT; ANGLIA ME SUSCEPIT; GALLIA ME DOCUIT; COLONIA ME TENET." *(Scotland bore me; England adopted me; France taught me; Cologne holds me.)*

Visit Duns Castle Country Park, the Jim Clark Museum (a memorial to the late world champion racing driver), and nearby Manderston House.

July sees the "Duns Reiver" leading the Riding of the Bounds, and August the County Agricultural Show.

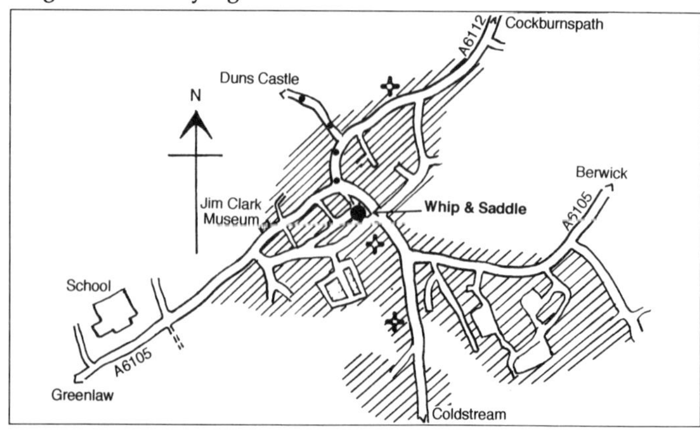

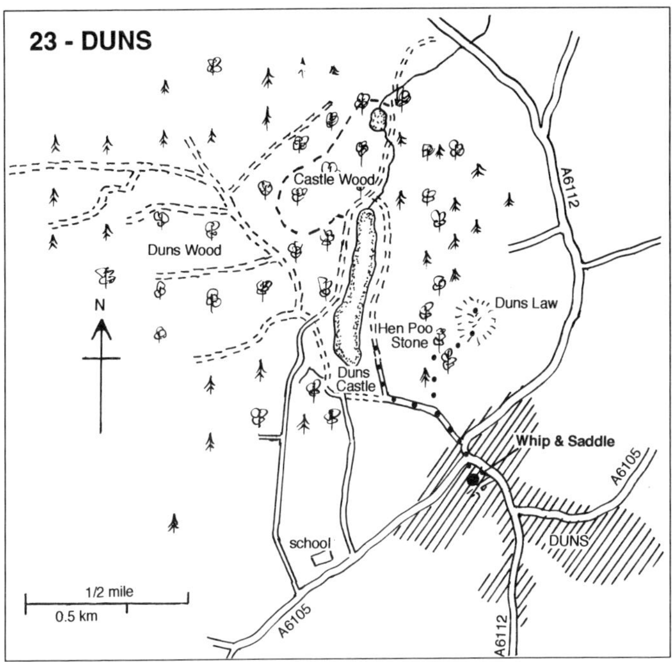

WALKS

A pleasing selection of five walks are available, in the country park surrounding Duns Castle, and on nearby Duns Law. From the Whip and Saddle walk N onto the A6112 and continue up Castle Sreet to a lodge gate marked "Duns Castle Estate". Just beyond the trees on the right a signposted path rises to Duns Law with its Covenantor's Stone, site of Old Duns and fine views. A great favourite with the dogs of Duns!

Carry on the tarmac road to the ornate gateway to Duns Castle, swing right past a memorial marking the birth-place of Duns Scotus to the lake known as "Hen Poo" - the castle lake. From here the ways are for walkers only, a noticeboard details the choices. The lake with its many inhabitants and pleasing surrounds delights the eye, in particular the rhododendrons in May and June. For the purist these walks may be a little too well manicured, if so the nearby Lammermuirs are recommended.

MOREBATTLE

24. TEMPLEHALL INN - Main Street, Morebattle, by Kelso TD5 8QQ. (01573) 440249 ***Colour photo opposite p64***

Morebattle, a pleasing sunny Scots village in the eastern Cheviots, is 8 miles (12.8km) south of Kelso via the B6436 and 4½ miles (7.2km) south-west of Yetholm on the B6401. The Templehall Inn stands at the east end opposite the kirkyard.

SITUATION *OS Map Landranger. Sheet 74 1:50,000 GR 772248*

The Templehall Inn stands between two decayed churches and derives its name either from Morebattle's association with the "Knights Templar", or its proximity with three of "God's Houses". Originally it was, until this century, a dairy farm selling not only the produce of its byre, but also the produce from the brewery.

The exterior, white with black margins, has one door leading into a passage

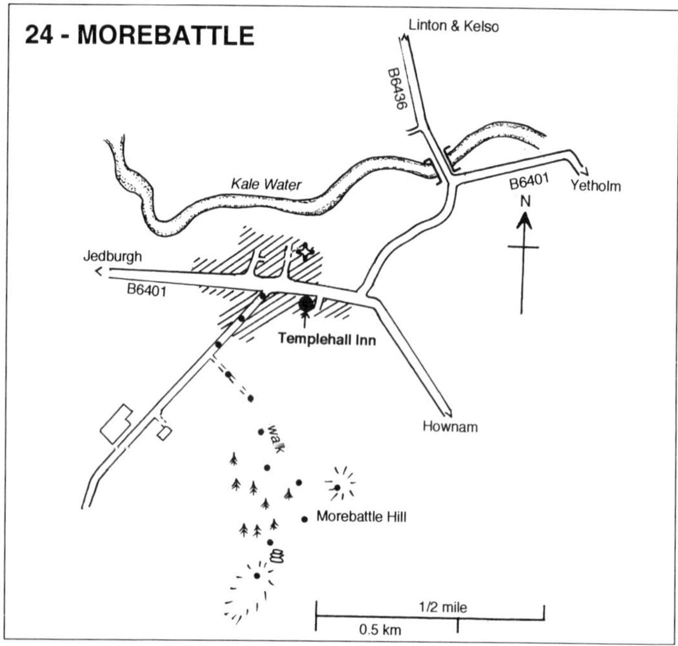

displaying tourist information and local notices; snug to the left, pool room to the right and ahead the bar. A small L-shaped room, with walls of sturdy girth, it wriggles over an uneven lino covered floor past a curved counter into the pool room. A journey that is dominated by a giant of a brown trout, 8lb 7½oz, taken from Kale Water. This small bar is not for the solitary drinker. A large lounge bar, open only at weekends and for functions, is accessed via a side door.

OPEN:	Winter, 11am-2.30pm, 5-11pm (Friday and Saturday 12 midnight) Summer, 11am (Sunday 12.30pm)-11pm (Friday and Saturday 12 midnight)
TYPE:	Free House
ON DRAUGHT:	McEwan's 80/-, 70/-, 60/- and Pale Ale, Younger's Tartan Special, Murphy's Irish Stout, Dry Blackthorn Cider
BOTTLED:	Newcastle Brown Ale, Younger's No 3, McEwan's 90/-, 80/-, Carlsberg Special Brew, plus stouts, lager and cider
WHISKY:	Prorietary blends and a few malts
WINE:	House, dry white; red; list of popular wines
FOOD:	In the bar and the snug, 11am-2.30pm, 5-9.30pm. Parties by arrangement
ACCOMMODATION:	2 twin, 1 family, 1 public bathroom
FACILITIES:	Pool room, darts, dominoes, bandit, juke box, music night - Saturday. Fishing permits - trout/greyling available
OPEN FIRES:	In lounge bar
WALKERS:	Welcome, parties asked to book
CHILDREN:	Children's licence, but not in the bar
DOGS:	Welcome, but not in vicinity of food
PARKING:	At the front and side of the inn

FOOD

Home cooked, from quality produce, obtained locally. Beef and Guinness pie a favourite. Children and vegetarians catered for.

ITEMS OF LOCAL INTEREST

Morebattle (Anglo-Saxon "botl", or abode by the mere or lochan) belonged to Glasgow Cathederal in the 1100s, the existing parish church was constructed in 1757 and dedicated to St Lawrence. A well, known as "Lawrie's Well", is situated below the kirkyard, close to the inn.

Nearby Linton, whose church is the oldest in use in Scotland and built not on rock but a heap of sand, is well worth a visit. The carved panel above its door portrays Sir John Somerville (knighted by William the Lion 1165-1214) slaying a "ravening beast".

The Wode Laird of Lariestone,
Slew the wode worm of Wormieston,
And sa gat all the lands of Linton paroshine.

Anon.

WALKS

A pleasant evening stroll, ascending Morebattle Hill, will reveal the Cheviots and the Kale Valley at their rolling best. Walk SW along Mainsfield Avenue, once past the houses turn left at the first gate to follow a cart track S as it ascends for 1/2 mile (0.80km) to the trig point on Morebattle Hill. Fine views from the twin summits, capped by the remains of a pre-historic fort and settlement, are the walker's reward. Descent can be E via a hunting gate onto Sybil's Path, a cart track to the road; or SE to Corbett tower and a road walk N of nearly a mile.

Many fine walks from nearby Hownam and Greenhill are detailed in *The Border Country - A Walker's Guide* by Alan Hall, Chapter 1.

KELSO

25. QUEENS HEAD HOTEL - Bridge Street, Kelso, Roxburghshire TD5 7JD. (01573) 224636. Fax (01573) 224459

Kelso stands at the junction of Tweed and Teviot in the heart of Tweeddale, where the A698, A699, A6089, B6350, B6352 and B6461 meet. The Queens Head is on the east side of Bridge Street, halfway between the Tweed bridge and Kelso's striking town square.

SITUATION *OS Map Landranger. Sheet 74 1:50,000 GR 728338*

Established in 1725, in the centre of the ancient market town, this Georgian coaching inn originally bore the name "Kings Head". Traditionally built with ample accommodation for travellers; ostlers and coachmen were quartered nearby. Today the Queens Head, with its white harled frontage and painted margins, is instantly recognizable. The small and friendly bar, its walls full of international sports shirts, snaps of happy customers and notices of sporting/social events, displays an array of good ale and shining bottles suggesting this room is more than just a bar. The adjoining lounge bar is long and spacious, a carpeted room full of atmospheric prints of Border life and death; with ample tables, cushioned wall settles and window seats, plus a specials blackboard above the red-brick fireplace. A maze of corridors and staircases lead to a pleasant dining room, a spacious functions room and the bedrooms, but not to the ghosts next door!

Kelso - Queens Head Hotel

OPEN:	Sunday to Thursday, 11am-2.30pm, 5-11pm Friday and Saturday, 11am-12 midnight
TYPE:	Free House
ON DRAUGHT:	Boddingtons Best Bitter, Whitbreads Castle Eden Ale, Theakston XB, Theakston Best Bitter, McEwan's 70/-, McEwan's Tartan Special, Guinness, Gillespies Malt Stout, Carlsberg Lager, McEwan's Lager, Autumn Gold Cider
BOTTLED:	Newcastle Brown Ale, Carlsberg Special Brew, plus a wide selection of lagers, stout and cider
WHISKY:	Proprietary blends and 35 chosen malts, including one on an optic
WINE:	House white, dry/medium; red. Thoughtful wine list of 30
FOOD:	Bar meals and dining room, 12 noon-2pm, 6-9.15pm. Menu handwritten and printed, plus 3 specials blackboards
ACCOMMODATION:	3 double 3 twin 2 family 3 single - 9 en-suite, 2 public facilities
FACILITIES:	Pool, darts, dominoes, bandit, quiz machine, tumble drier
OPEN FIRES:	Lounge bar
WALKERS:	Welcome, with cyclists, fishers, shooters
CHILDREN:	Welcome, in the eating areas
DOGS:	Welcome, not in the eating areas
PARKING:	Street parking or Abbey Row car park

FOOD

A full and varied menu of home cooked dishes to suit all tastes. Using fresh local produce, with an emphasis on game, fish and home-made sauces, dishes such as Sonsie mushrooms, Smailholm pie and Border game pie emerge from the kitchen to please the most critical palates.

ITEMS OF LOCAL INTEREST

Kelso, of Cymric origin ("calch myaydd" - chalkhill) by the junction of Tweed and Teviot with its 1128 Benedictine Abbey, neighbouring castle of Floors, fine airy square, elegant Town House, and Rennie's graceful five-arched Tweed Bridge, has an air of quiet gentility.

Host to, The Border Union Agricultural Show, Scottish Dog Show, Kelso Races, Kelso Civic Week, Kelso Ram Sales, rugby, golf, cricket, soccer and ice rink.

WALKS

A circular 4½ miles (7.2km) in 2¼ hours, scenically and historically appealing, the walk starts on the cobbles of Kelso Square. 30yds into Roxburgh Street turn left at "The Cobby" waymark, N with the glistening Tweed to a hard road which is followed to the gilded gates of Floors

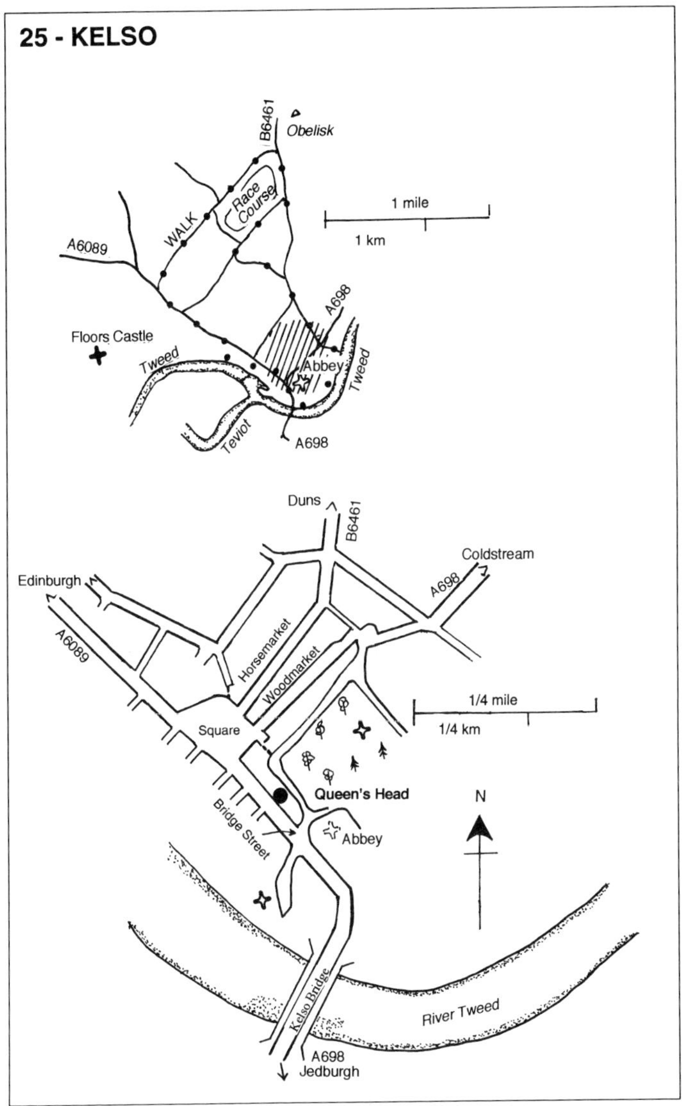
25 - KELSO
B6461
Obelisk
Race Course
WALK
1 mile
1 km
A6089
A698
Floors Castle
Tweed
Abbey
Tweed
Teviot
A698
Duns
B6461
Coldstream
A698
Edinburgh
A6089
Horsemarket
Woodmarket
1/4 mile
1/4 km
Square
Queen's Head
N
Bridge Street
Abbey
Kelso Bridge
River Tweed
A698
Jedburgh

Castle. Continue N by the "Dukes Dyke" wall to the east Lodge, then right following the sign E to Kelso racecourse. Ahead, underlined by an avenue of Lombardy poplar, stands "James Thomson's Obelisk". Continue E, past the grandstands/golf course, to the main road. Right and right again at the bridleway traversing the golf course, then left to the ice rink. Descend with the road and beyond the fire station fork left to Dryinghouse Lane crossroads. Directly ahead is the silvery Tweed which is followed west to Rennie's Bridge and the ruined abbey at journey's end.

Details of Town Trails from the TIC.

GREENLAW

26. THE CASTLE INN HOTEL - High Street, Greenlaw, Duns, Berwickshire TD10 6UR. (01361) 810217. Fax (01361) 810500

Dreaming of former glories, Greenlaw sits astride the crossroads of the A697 and the A6105; 9 miles (14.4km) north of Kelso and 10½ miles (16.8km) north-west of Coldstream. The four square Castle Inn Hotel stands centrally set back from the A697.

SITUATION *OS Map Landranger. Sheet 74 1:50,000 GR 712459*

Built as a hotel in 1831/5 by Lord Marchmont, on the site of an eighteenth-century inn, the Castle has retained its name and solid character. It was a stopping place for the many char-à-banc that travelled north/south in the first half of this century, 30 per day stopping for fuel and passengers' refreshment. When the omnibus traffic declined in the 1960s so did the Castle; a trend fortunately arrested in recent years.

The present welcoming proprietors have ensured The Castle Inn retains its spacious grandeur, albeit a little battle-scarred in places, by emphasising character coupled with good food. Gilt bannister rails guard spacious staircases, ticking wall clocks hypnotise, settees get lost in huge rooms with 12ft doors and 18ft high ceilings enlarged by gargantuan mirrors. The snug, with local sporting photographs, the spacious lounge bar and seated side rooms with their liberal scattering of prints are all ideal for restful reflection, but not with boots on.

OPEN:	12 noon-2.30pm, 6.30-11pm (Saturday, 12 midnight)
TYPE:	Free House
ON DRAUGHT:	Greenmantle Ale, Caledonian 80/-, Deuchers IPA, Younger's Tartan Special, Murphy's Irish Stout, Carlsberg Hof, Tennent's Lager, Gaymers Old English Cider

Greenlaw - The Castle Inn Hotel

BOTTLED: Selection of beer, stout, lager and cider

WHISKY: Proprietary blends and a careful selection of around 30 malts representing the flavours of Scotland

WINE: House white, dry/medium; red. List of European wines

FOOD: From a specials blackboard and over-all menu; bar, 12 noon-2.30pm, 6.30-10pm. Dining room times the same

ACCOMMODATION: 5 double/twin, 1 family; 2 en-suite, 4 shared facilities

FACILITIES: Non-electronic bar games in the snug. Resident's laundry

OPEN FIRES: Snug, lounge and big room

WALKERS: Welcome, please respect carpeted rooms

CHILDREN: Welcome

DOGS: Welcome from 3 residents

PARKING: Spacious park at front entrance

FOOD

The pride taken in presenting local dishes from fresh local produce is evident and emphasised by the range of home-made soups, including a rather special onion soup and cullen skink. Any dish, any room.

ITEMS OF LOCAL INTEREST

Greenlaw originally stood on the "Green Law" or hill, a mile or so south-east. The Mercat Cross erected in 1696 was pulled down in 1829 and cast aside, fortunately recovered in 1881 in the old church tower (once the town gaol). The old county hall indicates that Greenlaw was once the county town of Berwickshire, a dignity now lost.

The section of the Berwickshire Railway linking St Boswells and Duns was opened at Greenlaw in 1863, merging in 1876 with the North British Railway Company. It met a "Beecham's" end in the 1950s.

WALKS

A circular 8 miles (12.8km) walk with extensive views and a profusion of wildlife. From the Castle walk E via East High Street, then left to Marchmont Road chicken-sheds. Swing right to the old railway track which is followed E by the waters of Blackadder. After 1 mile (1.6km) the tree-lined way is blocked by scrub and a road, swing right via a small pasture to the road. For a shortened walk swing left at the road heading N to the T junction then left for Greenlaw.

Rejoin the old line, pass a sandstone bridge, winding N and E on embankments and rock clad cuttings for 2 miles (3.2km). The rail track ends by rusting agricultural implements; turn sharp left ascending a drive to Marchmont House. At the first buildings turn right (NW) crossing the carriageway below the fine frontage of Marchmont, before turning left (W). At the cattle grid swing right, between mounds of rhododendron, onto a country lane, returning to Greenlaw between manicured beech hedges (note the southern skyline).

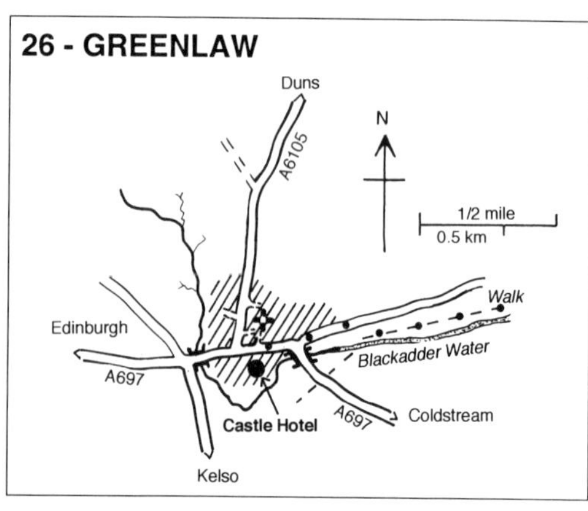

WESTRUTHER

27. THE OLD THISTLE INN - Westruther, Gordon, Berwickshire TD3 6NA. (01578) 740275.
The hamlet of Westruther stands by the B6456, 2½miles (4km) north-east of the A697 - GR 602476, and 11½ miles (18.4km) west of Duns, via the A6105 and the B6456. The Thistle is on the north side of the junction.

SITUATION *OS Map Landranger. Sheet 74 1:50,000 GR 633500*
Established in 1721 to serve the rural community, the "Old Thistle Inn" stands next to the old ruined kirk in the centre of Westruther, on the southern fringes of the Lammermuir Hills. Its white-washed harled exterior does not easily catch the eye of those who hurry by, but for those who have time to pause this local is a satisfying stop. The tiny beamed bar peppered with agricultural memorabilia leaves scant room for little else except pints (the most popular drink) and conversation. Cushioned wall seats, the odd chair and standing room surround two focal points, the counter and the brick fireplace with its ornate wood panel and carved eagle. The wooden floor once graced the old county building in Greenlaw - that is when Greenlaw was Berwickshire's county town.

Behind the bar is a games room with access to the garden. To the left of the entrance passage is the lounge, also beamed and furnished with buttoned wall seats and countryside prints. An inn with a name for food.

OPEN: Monday to Friday, 12 noon-2.30pm, 5-11pm
Saturday and Sunday, 12 noon-11pm
TYPE: Free House
ON DRAUGHT: McEwan's Export, Younger's Tartan Special, McEwan's Lager
BOTTLED: Newcastle Brown Ale, Stouts, Carslberg Special Brew, Brodie's Lager, Brodie's Cider, Diamond White Cider
WINE: House, white, dry and medium; red. Small select list
WHISKY: Proprietary blends and one solitary malt
FOOD: Mid-day and evening (no food mid-day Monday and Tuesday) in the bar, lounge and dining room
ACCOMMODATION: 2 twin rooms with en-suite facilities
FACILITIES: Games room with pool table, darts, dominoes; garden with tables and chairs. Trestle table/bench seat at entrance
OPEN FIRES: In the bar, doubles as drying room for wet clothes
WALKERS: Welcome, as are cyclists
CHILDREN: Welcome, not in the bar
DOGS: In the bar only, on a lead
PARKING: Limited to the street fronting the pub

Westruther - The Old Thistle Inn

FOOD

A limited menu for the bar and lounge, and not much bigger for the dining room in the evening. What is listed, from soup and sandwiches to the speciality Aberdeen Angus steaks, is home-made from local produce, and is generous in quality and quantity.

ITEMS OF LOCAL INTEREST

Originally known as "Wolfstruther, the swamp of the wolves" and "a place of old which had great woods, with wild beasts, fra quhilk the dwellings and hills were designed, as Wolfstruther, Raecleuch, Hindside, Hartlaw and Harelaw". Ivy-clad ruins of a Covenanting Kirk, the base of "Vietch of Westruther" in the 1600s, stand behind the inn. North of Westruther towers Twin Law, 1467ft (447m), topped by Twinlaw Cairns in memory of two members of the Edgar family who died in conflict.

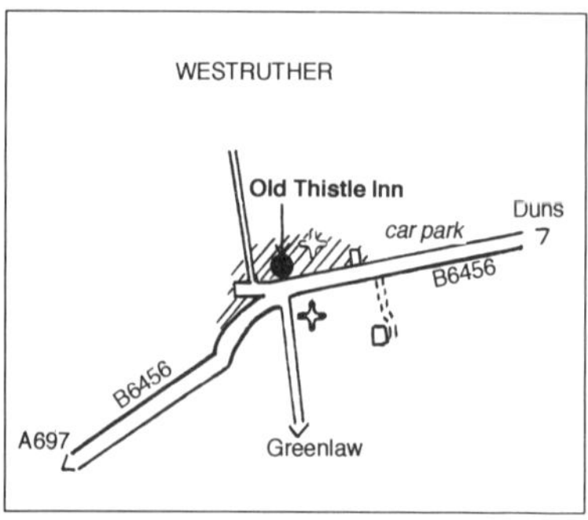

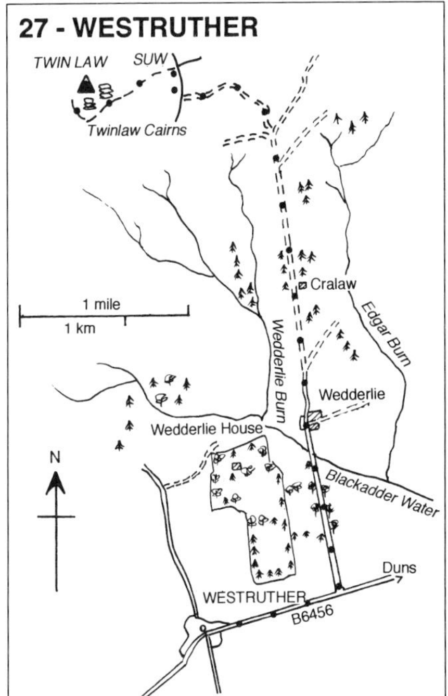

WALKS

The Southern Upland Way, crossing the Lammermuir Hills, can be joined at Twin Law or Watch Water reservoir, $4^1/_2$ miles (7.2km) N of Westruther. A good starting/ finishing point for an interesting few days.

A linear walk, of 9 miles (14.4km) ascending 771ft (235m) to Twin Law and back, is high in interest/views. E on B6456 to Wedderlie lane end, turn left (N) through an avenue of fine trees to Wedderlie Farm (bear left at the two forks ahead) onto twin concrete strips to Cralaw. A track over open fell leads to a gated wire fence, beyond the gate take the path left, rising W to the distinctive cairns of Twin Law. At the gated stone dyke ascend N with the wall to a SUW stile. Veer left, (W) with the Southern Upland Way (SUW) to the heathery summit, where the twin cairns provide a unique seat and viewing platform for the eastern Borders. Return to Westruther by the outward path.

ANCRUM

28. CROSS KEYS INN - The Green, Ancrum, Roxburghshire. (01835) 830344 *Colour photo opposite p65*

The floral village of Ancrum on the south bank of Ale Water is $^1/_2$ mile (0.8km) west of the A68(T) at the junction with the B6400; $4^1/_2$ miles (7.2km) north of Jedburgh and 6 miles (9.6km) south of St Boswells. The Cross Keys stands on the north side of the green.

SITUATION *OS Map Landranger. Sheet 74 1:50,000 GR 628245*
Ancrum, in a crook of Ale Water, its name derived from the ancient spelling of ale ("alne") and "Crom", Gaelic for crook, is a pleasing, quiet place. Set back from the road, the red sandstone Cross Keys with its distinct sign stands wedged in a row of village houses. Times have thankfully changed since 1878 - "I took up my lodgings for the night in a small miserable inn in the village of Ancrum; of which the people seemed alike poor and ignorant", (Tales of the Ettrick Shepherd). *Surely this must refer to the other village inn, now defunct!*

This friendly local, with its narrow passage, has but three small rooms, the bar, lounge bar and pool room. Their walls are half panelled with fine pine and the bar room counter is resplendent in grained pitch pine. A fine open fireplace and interesting old maps grace the lounge bar. It's a pub where conversation is instant and continuous. Space, though limited, is well used and service is smiling and swift. An open courtyard (coaching connections) stands at the back, where a covered walkway to the "gents" barely prevents a toilet prefix of "outside".

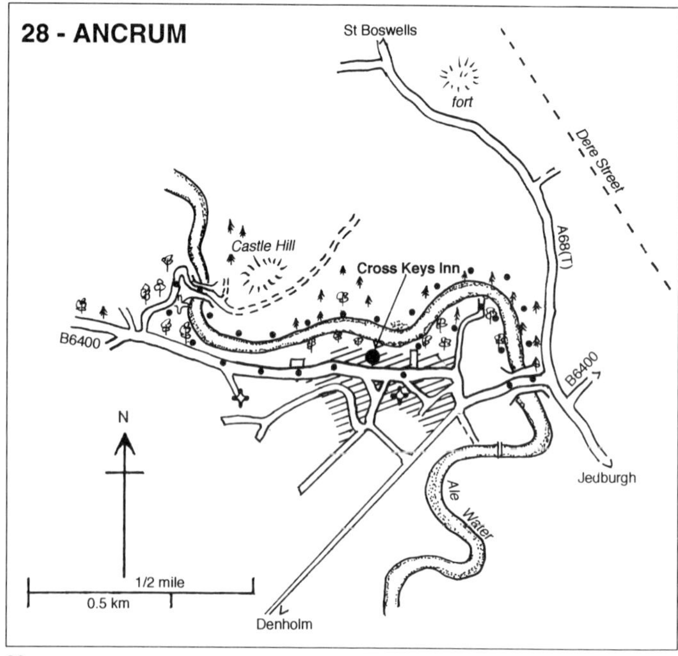

OPEN:	Monday to Wednesday, 6-11pm, Thursday, 6-12 midnight Friday, 12 noon-2.30pm, 5pm-12 midnight. Saturday, 12 noon-12 midnight, Sunday, 12.30-11.30pm
TYPE:	Free House
ON DRAUGHT:	Arrols 80/- Ale, Deuchers IPA, Dryborough's Heavy, Younger's Pale Ale, Guinness, Carlsberg Pilsner Lager
BOTTLED:	Newcastle Brown Ale, Carlsberg Special Brew, Guinness, Scrumpy Jack Cider plus a selection of lagers and stout
WHISKY:	Proprietary blends, Irish, de-luxe and selected malts
WINE:	House wine, white and red
FOOD:	Fresh-filled rolls and bar snacks only
ACCOMMODATION:	No
FACILITIES:	Darts, dominoes, bandit and pool table in pool room
OPEN FIRES:	Lounge bar
WALKERS:	Welcome
CHILDREN:	No
DOGS:	Under control
PARKING:	Limited, on the front apron

ITEMS OF LOCAL INTEREST

On the triangular green stands a thirteenth-century market cross of weathered red sandstone. North of the village, Ale *("white")* Water hurries between steep cliffs of red sandstone pock-marked with caves, one of which has the carving "James Thomson", author of *The Seasons*. Further north is Ancrum Moor, the battlefield where a pillaging English army was heavily defeated in 1545 by Leslie and Scott of Buccleuch.

Harestanes Countryside Visitor Centre, 1 mile east, provides a wealth of information plus four varied waymarked walks. Entrance free.

WALKS

A picturesque riverside and village stroll of 2½ miles (4km), with gentle ascents. W from the Cross Keys, past the parish church, for 700yds (640m) to a seat by a prepared path descending through trees. Continue by the kirkyard and ruined kirk to a packhorse bridge over the Ale Water. Beyond the bridge turn right onto a grassy track by the riverside fence, E with the winding Ale for ¾ mile (1.2km) (note the caves on the S bank and Castle Hill N), passing Ladies Well (wet underfoot) to clamber into a plantation high above a bend in the river. Descend S with care through the trees to Ale Bridge; cross the bridge to a footpath on the W bank and follow the Ale N to the Old Mill, taking the second pathway left into a snicket leading to the B6400 and Ancrum village green.

BONCHESTER BRIDGE

29. HORSE AND HOUND INN - Bonchester Bridge, Nr Hawick, Roxburghshire. (01450) 860645

Bonchester Bridge is a hamlet on the A6088, 5 miles east of Hawick and 8 miles west of Carter Bar. Bisected by the B6357, Kielder/Liddesdale to Jedburgh road. The Horse & Hound Inn is between the two bridges.

SITUATION *OS Map Landranger. Sheet 80 1:50,000 GR 586120*

This pleasant and welcoming inn began its working life as a coaching inn in 1704, known as "The Brig or Bridgend", it became Rule Valley's first post office on 11th May 1835. The then landlord's son, John Turnbull, whose grocer's shop was under the same roof, was appointed Rule Valley's first postmaster. The post office remained at the inn until 1907. It also had a smithy, up to the early 1900s, attached to its east gable, which is now the lounge bar. In the original building, the public bar is functional and friendly, with the added luxury of a coal fire in winter. The spacious lounge bar opens onto a small restaurant (no smoking), both tastefully and comfortably carpeted, furnished and hung with hunting scenes. Should the walker/cyclist mislay good manners and enter dripping wet, mine hosts (walkers themselves) will enquire if they may take the boots/outer garments to dry. In addition to a fine selection of real ale, the bar food and à la carte menu is interesting and the helpings large, even for the gourmet glutton.

OPEN:	*Summer*	*Winter*
	Monday to Saturday, 11am-11pm	Monday to Friday, 11am-2.30pm, 6.30-11pm
	Sunday, 12 noon-11pm	Saturday and Sunday, 11.30am-3pm, 5.30-12pm
	Closed Tuesdays.	
TYPE:	Free House	
ON DRAUGHT:	Orkney Dark Island, Greenmantle Ale, Deuchers IPA, Tetley Bitter, Carlsberg Export, Castlemains XXXX, Addlestones Cask Cider. Annual Beer Festival, 1st two weeks in May. Guest ales on bar blackboard	
BOTTLED:	Newcastle Brown, Wee Heavy, Becks, Carlsberg Special. Selection of beer, stout, lager and cider	
WHISKY:	Proprietary blends, 5 malts	
WINE:	House wine, white, dry and medium; red. Wine list - 13	
FOOD:	Lunch to 2pm, Evening 9pm. Bar menu and à la carte	
ACCOMMODATION:	2 double/family, 2 twin. H&C in 3 rooms, showers	

FACILITIES:	Restaurant, outdoor trestle tables (road side), drying room, darts, dominoes, tourist information
OPEN FIRES:	Bar and lounge bar in winter
WALKERS:	Welcome. Proprietors are enthusiasts
CHILDREN:	Welcome
DOGS:	Yes, but not in the lounge bar/restaurant
PARKING:	On three sides. Walkers' cars left by arrangement

FOOD

Five home-cooked specials on the blackboard add that little extra to the term pub grub. A speciality on Wednesdays and Saturdays is the "Greedy Gourmet Grill" - 12oz T bone - lamb chop - liver - gammon - chicken fillet - black pudding - sausage - chips - onions - peas. It's advisable to walk first!

ITEMS OF LOCAL INTEREST

Bonchester claims its name from the prominent hill above; it was named "Bona Castra" by the legions of Rome, and Bun Ceaster, the "reedy fortification" in old English. The dolerite summit of Bonchester Hill, 1060ft (323m) exhibits Iron Age ramparts and ditches, with

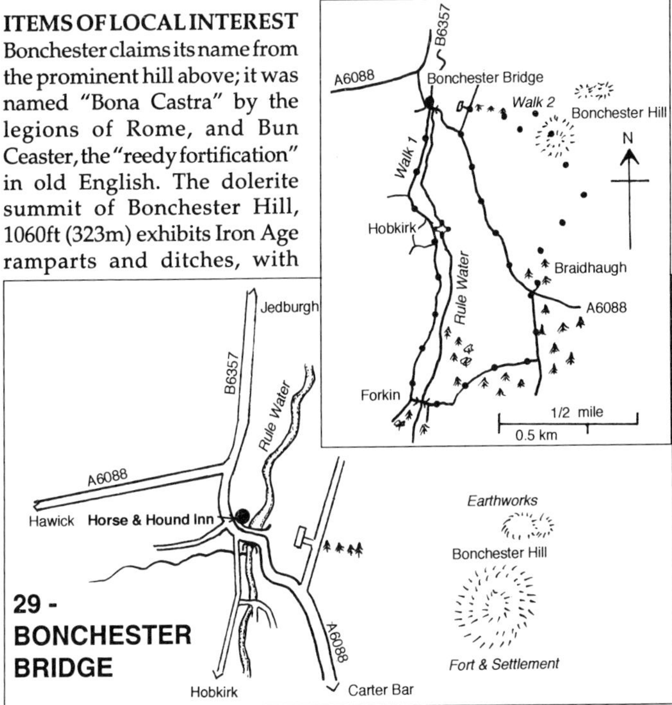

Bonchester Bridge - Horse and Hound Inn

evidence of a Roman occupation, and provides a superb viewing platform.

A visit to the red stone towered kirk at nearby Hobkirk is a must.

WALKS

1) Take the country lane to Hobkirk, for a $3^{1}/_{2}$ mile (5.6km) signposted stroll along tree-lined lanes close by the river-bank passing Hobkirk, Forkins and Cleuch Head to rejoin the A6088 to Bonchester Bridge.
2) Rise with the road S, swing left to Bonchester Farm. Turn right into a finger of conifers, ascending to open pasture and Bonchester Hill summit. The descent via a disused quarry follows a farm track to Braidhaugh caravan park then right onto the A6088 to Bonchester Bridge.

DENHOLM

The village of Denholm, in picturesque Teviotdale, is 5 miles (8km) east-north-east of Hawick on the A698. Both inns overlook the village green from the south side of the main street.

SITUATION *OS Map Landranger. Sheet 80 1:50,000 GR 568184*

Denholm - The Fox and Hounds Inn

ITEMS OF LOCAL INTEREST

Denholm ("DENUM" is an old English name meaning "at the valleys") stands by the confluence of Dean Burn and the River Teviot, watched over by the dark and brooding Ruberslaw, one of the most distinguished of Border hills. A busy community in 1849, it supported five inns plus a lady spirit dealer; today two inns remain.

Teviotdale, renowned for its little people and brownies, buried the last Denholm Witch at nearby Spital in the early 1600s. For sure she was a witch, for did not *"a cord break when her body was lowered into the grave and a robin redbreast alighted on the coffin"*.

In the 1700s flax grown on the common land was woven into linen cloth by the "wabsters" or weavers, the coarse fibres first being "retted" or softened in the Teviot or nearby "Geddholes".

Denholm Ba is an ancient Border's game. The "Ba" is said to represent an Englishman's head, and the match is between two teams, the "Uppies" (single men) and the "Doonies" (married men). The old jingle has it - "First comes Candlemas, then the new moon, the following Tuesday is Fasten E'en, the following Monday is Denholm Ba' Day".

Dr JOHN LEYDEN, born 1775, was the son of a Denholm shepherd; from the age of 15 he was awarded degrees in the arts, divinity and medicine. A friend of Walter Scott, he travelled abroad and from 1802 became a surgeon, a circuit judge and Professor of Languages in India. He died in Java aged 36. His monument on Denholm green was erected in 1861.

Landlord William Leyden, a "weel ken't" pedestrian in the 1860s walked to Innerleithen, took part in the games, and returned the same day: a round trip of 50 miles.

WALKS

1) The ascent to the craggy summit of Ruberslaw. Several routes offer the walker a journey of 2½ miles (4km) and an ascent of 1083ft (330m), from which the entire Scottish Borders can be viewed.

a) Ascend SE to Denholmhill Wood and Spital Tower, W to Ruberslaw Covert and S via Black Dod to the summit.

b) S by Woodside, then leave the road left (SE) to follow the woodland strip of Gled'swing Strip and Ruberslaw Covert via Black Dod to the rocky top.

c) SSW to Whiteriggs, left (E) onto the farm track by Hawk Burn and the plantation to the rocky outcrops by Peden's Pulpit.

2) A leisurely stroll in Denholm Dene, listed in 1898 as a holiday beauty spot. At the west end of the village green, beyond the Text House, turn right and enter the Dene via a stile opposite Denholm Lodge. The path crosses a bridge and follows the boundary of Honeyburn Farm, passing the site of the Rake, home of John Leyden's father in 1808. Recently several paths and bridges have been renewed.

30. THE FOX AND HOUNDS INN - Main Street, Denholm, Nr Hawick, Roxburghshire TD9 8NU. (01450) 870247. Fax (01450) 870500

Situated at the east end of Main Street, wedged between sandstone houses overlooking the village green. Three brisk paces take locals and visitors alike into the smallest of Border bars, its walls festooned with local notices, ale lists, bar mirrors, hunting scenes, old bottles, jugs and ale pots, a Horlicks machine and a world map mounted on the ceiling (for horizontal travellers). With two long tables and groaning settles by a cast iron fire, there is scant space for little more than pints and conversation in this busy bar, even though one customer once brought his horse in! At all times walkers are most welcome, their pints pumped, courtesy of "The Original Gaskell and Chambers Beer Engine", installed circa 1925. Leading from the bar is a long narrow lounge bar tastefully furnished, curtained and carpeted as befits an inn of character. The old stable courtyard, where previous proprietors kept a dog-cart, wagonette and horses for hire, has now been converted into a beer garden.

Tushielaw - Tushielaw Inn
Clovenfords - Clovenfords Hotel

Peebles - Glentress Hotel
Eskdalemuir - Hart Manor Hotel

OPEN:	Weekdays, 11am-2.30pm, 5-11pm Saturday and Sunday, - 11am-11pm
TYPE:	Free House
ON DRAUGHT:	Belhaven 80/-, Belhaven Best, Belhaven Light, plus several Real Ales. Murphy's Irish Stout, Tennent's Lager, Belhaven Lager, Addlestones Still Cider
BOTTLED:	Newcastle Brown Ale, Wee Heavy's, Carlsberg Special Brew. Selection of beers, stout, lager and ciders
WHISKY:	Teviotdale (Hawick distilled - no longer produced). Proprietary blends plus a selection of malts
WINE:	House, white and red from 11 selected wines

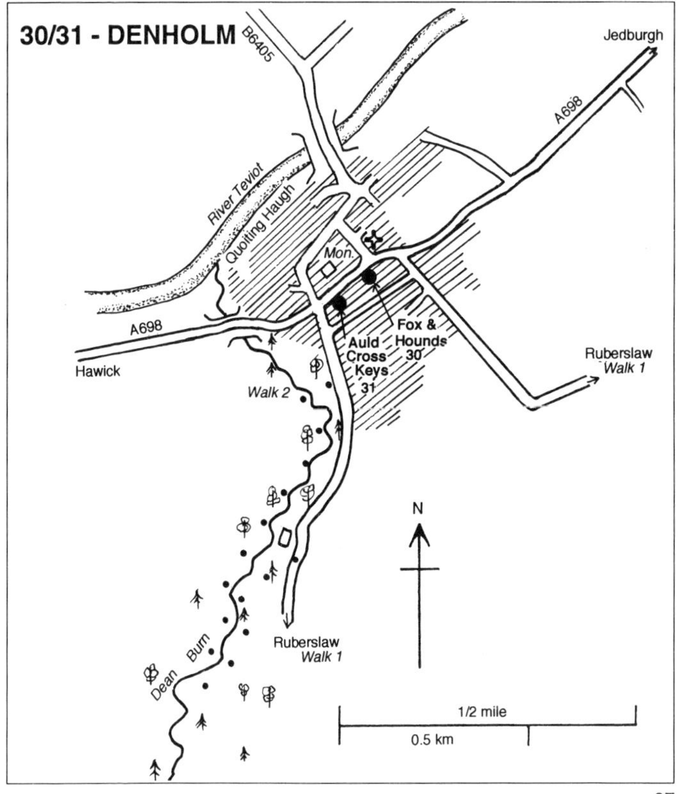

FOOD:	Lunch and evening, parties catered for, menu changed daily. Home-cooked specials
ACCOMMODATION:	1 family, 1 double, 1 single, all with H&C, 2 shared bathrooms. In the old stable premises.
FACILITIES:	Beer courtyard, stable games room with pool, darts, dominoes, cribbage, bandit
OPEN FIRES:	Bar, lounge bar and bedrooms
WALKERS:	Welcome
CHILDREN:	Welcome, but not in bar
DOGS:	Welcome, but bar space is limited
PARKING:	On the street and by the village green - limited

FOOD

A wide and varied choice of bar snacks to a full and satisfying meal are available midday and evening. Favourites with locals and visitors are the Fox's famous specials - steak and ale pie and death by chocolate pud.

31. THE AULD CROSS KEYS INN - Main Street, Denholm, Nr Hawick, Roxburghshire TD9 8NU. (01450) 870305

The attractive pebble-dashed exterior, bedecked with colourful flower baskets and a prominent inn sign, was built in the early 1800s as a bake house. It was first noted as an inn in Rutherford's Southern Counties Register of 1866, named "The Cross Keys Inn".

A small door opens directly into a functional wood-walled bar. Pictures of hunting scenes and past rugby triumphs provide wall decoration. Walkers are welcome on the lino floor, even with muddy boots. The main door leads into a comfortable well furnished lounge, where a small counter, an open fire and well decorated walls give a warm welcome. Glass doors and panels open out to connect with the dining room to the left, and a spacious functions room to the right. Walkers are also welcome here, but not in uniform.

An itinerant clairvoyant claimed a ghost named Harry stalks the cellar; to date Harry has not been experienced by others. Far more apparent is the life-sized figure of a Boy Blackamoor, dressed smartly in yellow, who on sunny days sits outside the bar door, on wet days inside.

OPEN:	Monday to Wednesday, 11am-2.30pm, 5-11pm, closed Mon am Thursday, 11am-2.30pm, 5-12 midnight Friday, 11am-2.30pm, 5pm-1am Saturday, 11am-12 midnight, Sunday 12.30-11pm
TYPE:	Free House
ON DRAUGHT:	Greenmantle Ale, Bass, Tennent's Special, Tennent's Light, J Aitken

Denholm - The Auld Cross Keys Inn

Special, Guinness, Dry Blackthorn Cider

BOTTLED: Selection of beers, stout, lager and cider

WHISKY: Proprietary blends, 10 malts

WINE: House white, dry and medium; red. Plus a list of 13, writ large on the lounge bar blackboard

FOOD: Lunch and evening meals in lounge bar and dining room. High teas on Sundays. Snacks and a daily specials board for bar only. Parties and functions catered for

ACCOMMODATION: No - arrangements can be made for B&B in the village

FACILITIES: Folk music club every 2nd Thursday, ceilidh singing, sponsor of quoit club on village quoiting haugh. Pool, darts, dominoes, bandit, TV

OPEN FIRES: Bar and lounge bar

WALKERS: Welcome

CHILDREN: Children's licence for lounge bar

DOGS: Allowed under control, away from food

PARKING: On main street frontage and at the rear

FOOD

At weekends an extensive lunch and evening menu for the lounge bar, with a choice of 30 main dishes, is certain to satisfy the most ravenous customer. The inn has received the Borders High Tea award.

MELROSE

32. BURTS HOTEL - Market Square, Melrose, Roxburghshire TD6 9PN. (01896) 822285. Fax (01896) 822870 ***Colour photo opposite p65***
The borders township of Melrose, with its ancient abbey, lies below the Eildon Hills and alongside the silvery Tweed; 3 miles (4.8km) east of Galashiels via the A6091. Burts Hotel graces the south side of the triangular market place in the town centre.

SITUATION *OS Map Landranger. Sheet 73 1:50,000 GR 539343*
The distinctive building of Burts Hotel was first erected in 1722, a private town house of some standing, and although time has altered its function it still retains that eighteenth-century style. In 1880 the Misses Anderson purchased the property and it became "Anderson's Temperance Hotel". In the 1930s Mr Burt, butler to the Earl of Haddington, took over, changing both name and use to Burts Hotel (with no apostrophe). Today the white rough-cast external walls give Burts an inviting appearance which extends throughout the premises, and is enhanced by the welcoming staff. The comfortable and carpeted lounge bar, with cushioned wall seats and windsor chairs, is bright and roomy; its walls tastefully adorned with fading sepia photographs, rural prints, brass and military memorabilia. A central open fireplace adds warmth. Two lounges and a spacious dining room complete the ground floor facilities.

OPEN:	Monday to Saturday, 11am-2.30pm, 5-11pm Sunday, 12 noon-2.30pm, 6-11pm
TYPE:	Free House
ON DRAUGHT:	Belhaven 80/- Ale, Courage Directors, Belhaven Best Bitter, Murphy's Irish Stout, Carlsberg Pilsner, Carlsberg Hof, Old English Cider
BOTTLED:	In addition to a selection of beer, stout and cider, Newcastle Brown Ale and Traquair Ale
WHISKY:	Proprietary blends, and as befits a member of the Scottish Malt Whisky Society, a comprehensive range of varied malts
WINE:	House wines - white, dry and medium; red and a claret; plus a thoughtful and selective wine list
FOOD:	Lounge bar - lunches/suppers, waitress service, 12 noon-2pm/6pm-9.30pm (Friday and Saturday 6pm-10.30pm). Dining Room - à la carte and table d'hôte menu changed daily, 12.30-2pm/7-9.30pm
ACCOMMODATION:	21 en-suite bedrooms, all with modern facilities
FACILITIES:	Billiards room (residents), garden with tables and chairs in summer, drying facilities (residents)

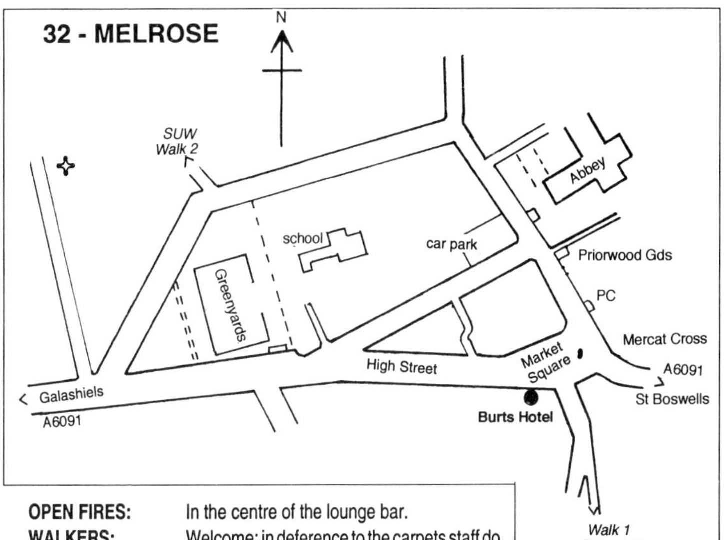

OPEN FIRES: In the centre of the lounge bar.
WALKERS: Welcome; in deference to the carpets staff do not object to stockinged feet
CHILDREN: Welcome, accompanied by an adult in the lounge bar
DOGS: Welcome
PARKING: Hotel car park, walkers' cars left by arrangement

FOOD

Specialising in local dishes with a difference, with game as the cornerstone. Home-made soups, paté/terrine, casseroles etc. are available alongside enticing presentations of salmon, beef, lamb and game.

ITEMS OF LOCAL INTEREST

Tourist Town of 1992, Melrose is a cornucopia of interest; its Cistercian abbey, founded 1136, provides humour as well as spiritual peace. Once renowned for quality lace, Melrose is the birthplace of "Rugby Sevens" (initiated at the Greenyards by butcher Ned Haigh). Visit Abbotsford House, Priorwood Gardens, Roman Trimontium and the Motor Museum.

WALKS

1) The Eildon Hills, $3^{1}/_{2}$ miles (5.6km), ascent 1148ft (350m), time

2 hours. S from the Mercat Cross, below the by-pass bridge to a sign "Eildon Walk". Ascend the waymarked steps and stiles to the open hillside, turning right to the col above. Ascend right on a steep path to the heathery summit of Eildon, the panorama will reward and enthral. Return to the col and ascend the NE Eildon, Iron Age/Roman forts and Roman vineyard. From the summit descend steeply E to the gorse, turn left contouring W to meet the outward path; retrace to Melrose.
2) Abbotsford House, 6 miles (9.6km), ascent 197ft (60m), time 3 hours. To the Greenyards (Melrose RFC), a waymarked SUW (Southern Upland Way) (thistle emblem) passes the parish church N to the riverside. Follow the Tweed W for 2 miles (3.2km) to the Waverley Line Bridge over the Tweed. Do not cross, descend to the river-bank and continue SW passing Lochend to the A6091. Cross onto a wooded track S for 500yds to Abbotsford (home of Sir Walter Scott); return via the scenic country lane that rises S beyond Abbotsford car park, then E via Kaeside and Sunnyside Farm to Darnick and Melrose.

LILLIESLEAF

33. CROSS KEYS INN - West End, Lilliesleaf, Roxburghshire TD6 9JA. (01835) 870310

Lilliesleaf, an attractive though lengthy village, is on the B6359; 8 miles (12.8km) south of Melrose and 8$^1/_2$ miles (13.6km) north from Hawick. The Cross Keys snuggles coyly into a row of houses at the west end bend.

SITUATION *OS Map Landranger. Sheet 73 1:50,000 GR 531249*
Originally called "Lilliesclive" in a twelfth-century charter, the village is picturesquely situated on a ridge above Kale Water, a village of gardens and flowers, a delight in summer. Pebble dashed walls, one front door and five leaded windows invite the traveller to this small and cheery local; bar on the right, lounge on the left. The part panelled and beamed bar, with evidence of "blackening" a whimsical local custom - on the ceiling, a cosy brick fireplace and just enough tables and stools, is popular with locals and visitors. The quaint lounge bar, its stone walls both bared and plastered, is even smaller and cosier, with a selection of 1877 photographs. Photographs show a coaching inn with a different appearance; sadly a major fire in the 1940s destroyed everything except sections of the outside walls.

OPEN:	Monday to Wednesday, 12 noon-2.30pm, 5-11pm
	Thursday and Friday, 12 noon-2.30pm, 5pm-12 midnight

	Saturday and Sunday, 12 noon-12 midnight, Sunday, open 12.30pm
TYPE:	Free House
ON DRAUGHT:	Boddingtons Best Bitter (Guest Real Ales listed on blackboard), McEwan's 70/-, Theakston XB, McEwan's Pale Ale, Gillespies Malt Stout, Harp Lager
BOTTLED:	Newcastle Brown Ale, Becks Bier, Carlsberg Special Brew, plus a selection of stouts, lager and cider
WHISKY:	Proprietary blends and 2 malts
WINE:	House white - dry and medium; Red. Plus a small wine list
FOOD:	In bar and lounge bar, 12 noon-2pm, 5-9pm. Bar snacks, eg. pizza, sandwiches, opening hours. Takeaway food 12 noon-2pm, 5-9pm
ACCOMMODATION:	No
FACILITIES:	Darts, dominoes, bar skittles, draughts, chinese checkers, backgammon, bandit, quiz nights
OPEN FIRES:	Coal stove in the bar, fire in lounge bar
WALKERS:	Welcome, as are all countryside enthusiasts
CHILDREN:	In lounge bar only with adult for food
DOGS:	Not in lounge bar
PARKING:	For 3 cars on front apron, otherwise street side

FOOD

Pleasantly different, changed daily specials are displayed on the bar blackboard. Also a good menu, using local produce (some from a neighbour's garden) when available, with the Border beef and beer casserole a firm favourite. Children and vegetarians catered for.

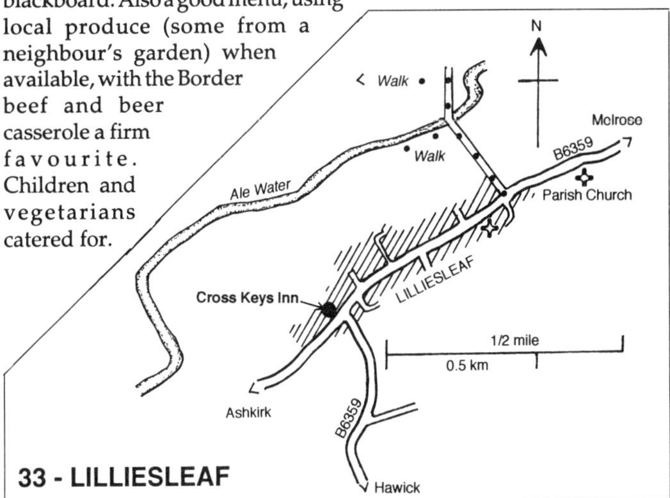

Lilliesleaf - Cross Keys Inn

ITEMS OF LOCAL INTEREST

At nearby Riddell, with its fine tubular Tower, a stone coffin bears the date A.D. 727. Lilliesleaf old church, said to have been built in the ninth century, belonged to the See of Glasgow, and later an annual sum of £5 7s 6$^{1}/_{2}$d, known as the "Bishop's Cat", was paid to the university of Glasgow. The parish church was restored in 1870, when the original Catholic font was recovered from a local mire, having been deposited there by over-zealous Reformers.

WALKS

Turn N onto a tarmac lane at the east end of the village and descend to a grassy picnic/play area by Ale Water. Two routes are available:

1) A narrow path winds W between fence and river-bank, home to flowers and birds. Pass an old farm steading to the football pitch, beyond which the farm road swings left to join the B6400 E to the Cross Keys.

2) For a fine walk via Riddell Tower, swing right to cross the footbridge, turning left beyond the house onto a farm track. For 1 mile (1.6km) the track ambles W and SW above Ale Water before reaching Riddell Tower (ascend by the trees to the tower). Continue SW with the track, swinging left at all junctions, crossing the bridge S to the B6400, E with the road for a mile, via a sawmill, to Lilliesleaf.

LAUDER

34. EAGLE HOTEL - Main Street, Lauder, Berwickshire TD2 6SR. (01578) 722426 or 722255

The royal and ancient Burgh of Lauder stands on the A68(T) road and above Leader Water; the centre of picturesque Lauderdale surrounded by the hills of Lammermuir. North of the Town House the Eagle Hotel graces the east side of the main thoroughfare.

SITUATION *OS Map Landranger. Sheet 73 1:50,000 GR 531476*

A welcoming entry into this clean and bright local is made through two doors, directly from the street. The smaller bar, its walls hung heavy with old photographs, mirrors and adverts, is a cosy, friendly room, with a fine mahogany counter and a mirrored gantry, warmed by an open fire and a warm red ceiling. The long narrow bare stone walled lounge bar with its inglenook open fire has the most unusual bar counter in the Borders (a unique glass-fibre replica of an Elizabethan four poster bedhead). An inn much frequented by locals and visiting sportsmen.

Originally built in the mid 1600s as a minister's residence, it was later leased to the town baker and in the early 1800s became a coaching inn, one of

Lauder - Eagle Hotel

several on the Edinburgh to Newcastle route. Taking its name from the eagles who once circled the Lammermuir Hills, all that remains today is a wooden carving in the bar. Whispers concerning a ghostly presence in the Eagle have been reported.

OPEN:	Summer 11am-11pm; winter 11am-2.30pm, 5-11pm
TYPE:	Free House
ON DRAUGHT:	Wm McEwan 80/- Ale, John Smith's Bitter, Younger's No 3, Theakston Best Bitter, McEwan's 70/- Ale, Younger's Tartan Special, Murphy's Irish Stout, Carlsberg Export Hof Lager, McEwan's Lager
BOTTLED:	Newcastle Brown Ale, Becks Bier, Carlsberg Special Brew, Kaltenberg Pils, plus popular beers, stouts, lager, cider
WHISKY:	Proprietary blends and a fine selection of 40 malts
WINE:	House white - selection of 4 on chill, dry to sweet; red of medium quality. Small wine list
FOOD:	Served in the bar, lounge bar and dining room, 12 noon-2pm and 6-9pm
ACCOMMODATION:	5 bedrooms - 4 with wash basins and shower, shared toilet facilities. As from 1995 all en-suite
FACILITIES:	Darts, dominoes and bandit in the bar
OPEN FIRES:	Bar and lounge bar
WALKERS:	Welcome
CHILDREN:	Welcome in lounge bar and hotel
DOGS:	Allowed, but not where food is served
PARKING:	Public car parks alongside the hotel and by the Town House

FOOD

A regularly changed menu is available, including in-demand specials such as coq au vin and beef bourguignon. Despite the European influence local fresh ingredients are used. Parties catered for by arrangement and well patronised locally.

ITEMS OF LOCAL INTEREST

An ancient and royal burgh on the main route in/out of central Scotland, though small in size (population 800), Lauder is large in history and interest. Thirlestane Castle, family seat of the Earls of Lauderdale, is open to the public. The old bridge is where James III's nobles mutinied and hanged his "favourites"; and the old gaol where Napoleon's officers fought a duel with razors lashed to sticks.

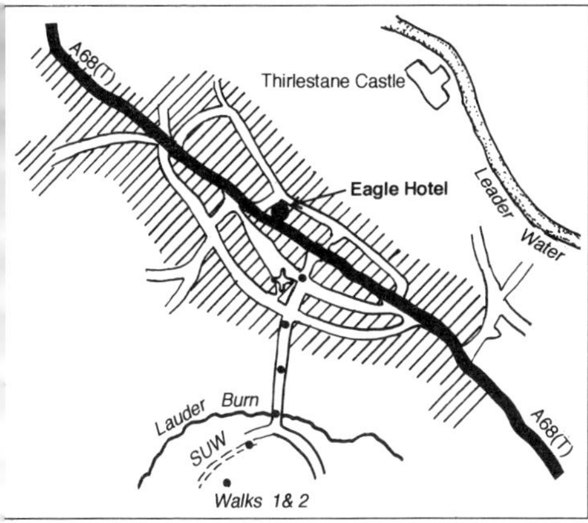

WALKS

The Southern Upland Way passes through Lauder, and the section above Lauder Burn forms one leg of a 6 mile walk over Lauder Common.

1) S on the SUW, via Mill Wynd and the Kirk to Burn Mill. Ascend the waymarked path SW by the golf course for 1 mile (1.6km), before descending steeply to Lauder Burn. Leave the SUW, turn left and ascend NNW with the plunging burn through a narrow defile (a little burn louping required) before passing through a stone dyke gate. At the meeting of pylons and poles take the cart track W over the heathery fell, crossing a hard road to an enclosed coniferous plantation.

Fine views before descending NE over Lauder Common to the main road. Turn right and right again onto Muircleugh road walking S, to return via the outward feeder burn to Lauder Burn which is followed NE. An old quarry can be seen above. Just beyond, ascend from the burnside to join the grassy quarry path by the ruins of a "checkers hut". Follow this path through banks of gorse and over footbridges to Lauder.

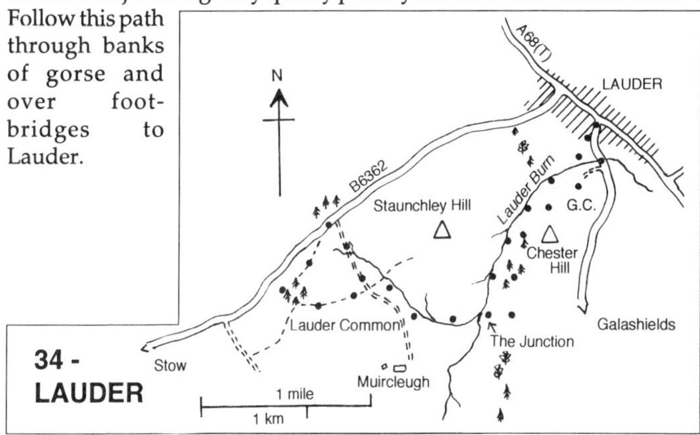

Chapter 3
Scottish Borders - West

OXTON

35. TOWER HOTEL - 3 Main Street, Oxton, Lauder, Berwickshire TD2 6PN. (01578) 750235

Ancient Oxton stands 1/2 mile (0.8km) west of the A68, signposted "Oxton" 1/2 mile (0.8km) north from Carfraemill. The Tower dominates the village crossroads in the centre of Oxton.

SITUATION *OS Map Landranger. Sheet 73 1:50,000 GR 496535*

A relatively modern inn by Border standards, the Tower was built in 1903; its title deeds insist it must remain as an hotel with its original name. Named after its prominent angular corner tower there is no mistaking this local with the white rough-cast walls.

Two doors open from the street; the smaller of the two on the left steps into the bar, proudly claiming the longest continuous wooden bar counter in the area, enlarged by the clever use of reflective mirrors and sparkling bottle gantries that catch the eye and tempt the palate. Add the warm burgundy decor, a friendly welcome, a roaring log/coal fire flanked by cushioned church pews, and you have a fitting end to a good walk. The adjoining lounge and dining room are comfortable, as are the three bedrooms, one of which is in the spacious corner tower.

OPEN:	Easter to October,	Monday to Wednesday, 12 noon-11pm
		Thursday to Sunday, 12 noon-12 midnight
	November to Easter,	Monday and Tuesday 5-11pm
		Wednesday, 12 noon-2pm, 5-11pm
		Thursday, 12 noon-2pm, 5-12pm
		Friday to Sunday, 12 noon-12 midnight
TYPE:	Limited "Tie", Scottish Brewers	
ON DRAUGHT:	Wm McEwan 80/-, Theakston Best Bitter, McEwan's Tartan Special, McEwan's Pale Ale, Guinness, Heineken Lager, McEwan's Lager, Strongbow Cider	
BOTTLED:	Selection of beers, stout, lager and cider	
WHISKY:	Proprietary blends and a small selection of malts	

WINE:	House red and white, medium
FOOD:	Dining room and lounge. Easter to October 12 noon to 8.30pm. November to Easter, midweek, opening hours to 8.30pm. Weekends all day to 8.30pm. Menus plus specials blackboard
ACCOMMODATION:	3 Doubles, (2 family rooms), share 1 bathroom/1 shower
FACILITIES:	Pool table, darts, dominoes, juke box and bandit in bar
OPEN FIRES:	Two fine fires, bar and lounge
WALKERS:	Most welcome, along with other outdoor enthusiasts
CHILDREN:	Welcome in the lounge and dining room
DOGS:	Welcomed by the staff, but not the resident Alsatian
PARKING:	Limited, streetside parking

FOOD

One of the Tower's main attractions is the home-cooked local dishes. Top of the list are home-made soups, liver and onions, home-made steak pie, and on Sundays, roast beef and Yorkshire puddings.

ITEMS OF LOCAL INTEREST

"The villa of Ulfkiliston", referred to in the charter of Alan

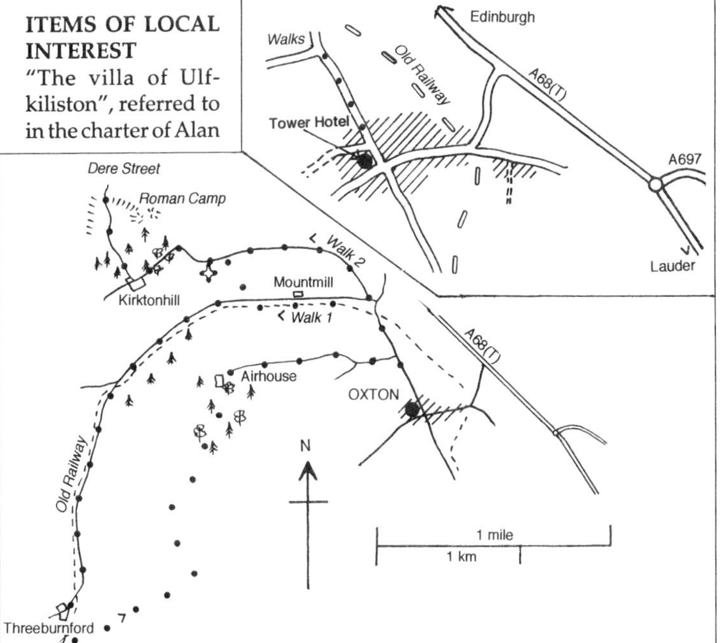

Oxton - Tower Hotel

of Galloway (1200-1234), was changed to Ugstoune in the fifteenth century and to Oxton in the nineteenth. Channelkirk, 2 miles (3.2km) north-west of Oxton, was a first-century Roman station on the lifeline of Dere Street.

In the kirkyard of Channelkirk church there is a metal-framed coffin guard, used to protect recently interred cadavers from the ghoulish activities of Burke and Hare, who occasionally ventured over Soutra Hill in search of saleable samples for the Edinburgh Faculty of Surgeons.

WALKS

1) Oxton, N to the old railway track then left and W by Mountmill Burn then S through the tight and picturesque valley to Threeburnford. At this ancient crossing place swing left at the small plantation to take the winding and ascending path NE for 1½ miles (2.4km) to Airhouse. Pass through the avenues of trees turning E, to rejoin the road to Oxton.

2) Oxton, N on the signposted road to Kirktonhill, swinging right at the farm cottage, where a farm track leads beyond the narrow plantation onto the hill housing Channelkirk Roman camp and the distinct remains of Dere Street. Fine views S into Lauderdale; return via the outward route.

NEWCASTLETON

36. THE LIDDESDALE HOTEL - Newcastleton, Roxburghshire TD9 0QD. (013873) 7255

Newcastleton centred in isolated Liddesdale stands on the B6357 alongside Liddle Water. 10½ miles (16.8km) north of Canonbie and 18¼ miles (29km) south of Hawick. The Liddesdale Hotel in the central square is west of the main road.

SITUATION *OS Map Landranger. Sheet 79 1:50,000 GR 482876*

The "town" of Newcastleton, named after the old village of Castleton, sprang up in 1793, built by the then Duke of Buccleuch as a weaving centre. Its long main street is broken at regular intervals by small set back squares. The Liddesdale became a coaching inn after 1800, when Sir Walter Scott drove his gig into the dale, the first wheeled vehicle to travel into Liddesdale. Nearby stables and outhouses indicate its coaching inn status. First impressions of the inn's exterior suggest formality, the welcome, however, in this family-run inn is as warm as the summer's sun. A wood-panelled friendly bar with cushioned benches, 120 shining miniatures and lino on the floor leads, via two steps, into the cosy lounge bar, open fire, old prints, maps et al. A charming breakfast/dining room seating ten, all lace and rural prints, adjoins the bar; for larger parties a functions room up the stair caters for 60. A room that has witnessed generations of local weddings.

Newcastleton - The Liddesdale Hotel

OPEN:	Summer, 11am-11pm, Friday and Saturday 12 midnight Winter, 11am-2.30pm, 6-11pm, Friday and Saturday midnight
TYPE:	Free House
ON DRAUGHT:	Belhaven Best, McEwan's 70/-, Younger's Tartan Special, Younger's Pale Ale, Gillespies Malt Stout, Tennent's Lager, Strongbow Dry Cider
BOTTLED:	Newcastle Brown Ale, Carlsberg Special Brew, Diamond White Cider, plus standard beers, stout, lager and cider
WHISKY:	Proprietary blends, 8 malts in summer
WINE:	House white, dry and medium; red. A wine list of 18
FOOD:	Bar and dining room menus; 12 noon-2pm, 7-9pm
ACCOMMODATION:	2 double, 2 twin, 1 family, with private bath/shower
FACILITIES:	Bandit, quiz machine, darts, dominoes, drying room
OPEN FIRES:	1 in lounge bar
WALKERS:	Welcome, mine host is an enthusiast
CHILDREN:	Welcome in the hotel, not in the bar
DOGS:	Welcome

FOOD

Prepared from fresh Liddesdale meat, fish and vegetables (vegetables a speciality) the choice is pleasing and the dishes satisfying. Saturday night specials and Sunday roasts are on a seperate menu.

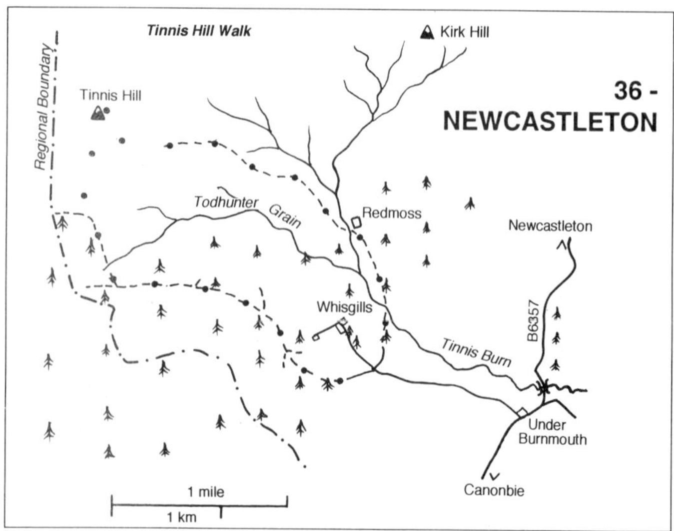

ITEMS OF LOCAL INTEREST

Two prominent families (clans) of Border reivers dwelt in Liddesdale, the Armstrongs and the Elliots; families that are enshrined in border history and legend.

> *On the Border was the Armstrongs, able men,*
> *somewhat unruly, and very ill to tame.*
>
> Satchells

Nearby stands Larriston, family stronghold of the Elliots, and on the site of the old railway station there stood the Pele of Park, tower of Little Jock Elliot, the very same who tangled with Queen Mary's Bothwell.

> *My name is little Jock Elliot,*
> *And whar daur meddle wi' me?*
>
> Anon

Visit Hermitage Castle and the Armstrong Museum. A Traditional Music Festival is held in July, in August the Liddesdale Agricultural Show.

WALKS

1) A riverside and town walk is signposted from various points on the main street. The return can be via the old rail line reached by the bridge N of the town.

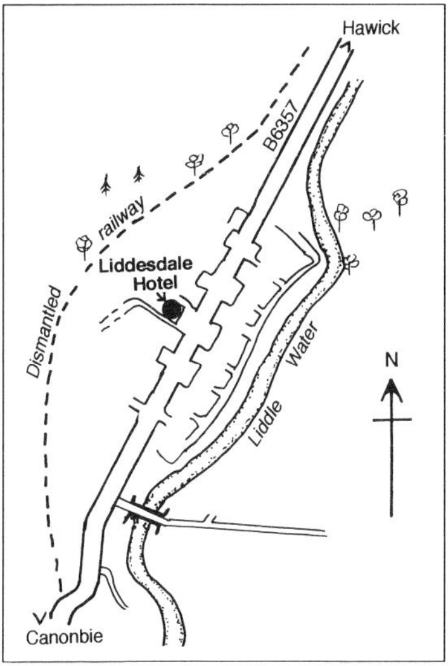

2) The ascent of Tinnis Hill 1325ft, (404m). A circular walk of $5^{1}/_{2}$ miles (8.8km), from the forest road at GR 454832. Ascend NW via Whisgills Edge and Windy Edge, then N alongside the conifers onto the open fell (can be wet) to Tinnis Hill summit (a superb grandstand). Descend E onto a cart track, between the gullies of Tinnis and Todhunter Burns, to Redmoss. And finally SE through the conifers to GR 454832.

Further walks are described in Liddesdale Walks leaflets.

SELKIRK

37. THE CROSS KEYS INN - 25 Market Place, Selkirk TD7 4BL. (01750) 721283

Standing proudly above Ettrick Water, the mill town of Selkirk is at the junction of the A699, A7(T), A707, A708 and B7009. The Cross Keys Inn is situated on the east side of the market place.

SITUATION *OS Map Landranger. Sheet 73 1:50,000 GR 471284*

The Cross Keys, housed in what was a nineteenth-century post office, is flanked by the old courthouse and overlooked by Sir Walter Scott; ideally placed for the annual "Casting of the Colours". The off-white frontage and coloured bow windows carry a colourful inn sign of gold and silver crossed keys above the single door leading into the small and busy bar. Boots present no problems with the lino floor, and if the legs are tired cushioned wall seats relieve the strain. A shining, friendly place where fading photos rub shoulders with USA car plates.

The carpeted lounge bar is a "step-up" from the bar, its walls lined with buttoned seats and tidy tables. Up the stair a wee snug seats 15; off the lounge bar, built into an old close, the narrowest and longest "gent's loo" in the borders, fondly referred to as the "Yer-needin Line, a single track with no passing places"!

Success to the Keys-
Wi' attractions like these,
Nae bye-laws are needed to keep us in order;
Whene'er we think lang
For a drink an' a sang,
We'll trek for the liveliest pub on the Border!
Anon

OPEN:	Sunday, 12.30-11pm, Monday to Wednesday, 11am-11pm Thursday to Saturday, 11am-12 midnight
TYPE:	Free House
ON DRAUGHT:	Caledonian 80/-, Cross Keys (Dryboroughs) 70/- Ale, Tetley Bitter, Alloa Light, Guinness, Carlsberg Export, Carlsberg Lager, Castlemain XXXX, Gaymer's English Cider
BOTTLED:	Boddingtons Ale, Newcastle Brown Ale, Carlsberg Special Brew, plus a selection of beer, stout, lager and cider
WHISKY:	Proprietary blends, 12 representative malts
WINE:	House white on tap, medium; red
FOOD:	Bar lunch 12 noon-2.30pm, supper, 6.30-9pm (not Saturday)

Selkirk - The Cross Keys Inn

ACCOMMODATION: Proprietor has B&B, 5mins from Cross Keys
FACILITIES: Dominoes, bandit, quiz machine, juke box, match-days TV
OPEN FIRES: No
WALKERS: Welcome, as are all outdoor enthusiasts
CHILDREN: In eating areas, lounge and upstairs snug
DOGS: Under control and on a lead
PARKING: In the market place and nearby Halliwell's car park

FOOD

Frequent winners of the SBTB Award - Best Bar Food. Home-made bar meals using fresh produce wherever possible, four varied daily specials, such as "Desperate Dan's Steak Pie", in great demand; all dishes are big on quality and quantity. Children, OAPs catered for.

ITEMS OF LOCAL INTEREST

The Common Riding festival is the oldest in the Borders, tracing its origins to Flodden Field 1513 and Fletcher, the sole survivor from a troop of 80, who returned - with an English banner.

In 1745 the Souters (shoemakers) of Selkirk made 2,000 pairs for Bonnie Prince Charlie's south-bound tramping army; and for their pains received not one penny piece. The insignia and documents of the ancient Craft of Cordiners are still preserved in the old courtroom of Sir Walter Scott, Sheriff for 33 years - open to the public and adjacent to The Cross Keys.

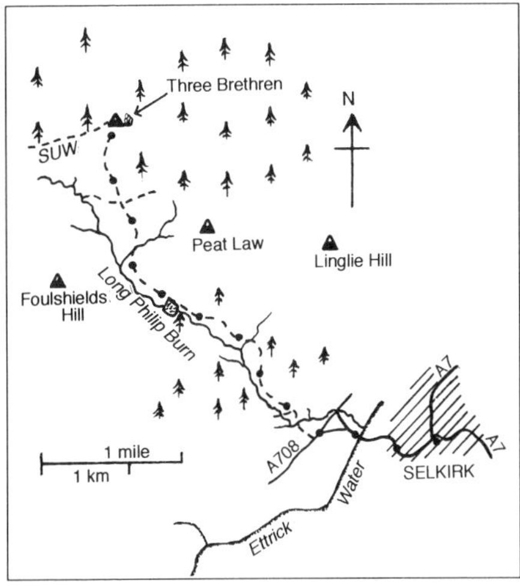

WALKS

An energetic hill walk of 8 miles (12.8km) ascending 1132ft (345m) to the charismatic grandstand of the Three Brethren. Cross the Ettrick Bridge and pass the rugby ground to Philiphaugh Farm. Turn right (NW) onto the farm road and follow Long Philip Burn through forest and by Corbie Linn to a small reservoir to reach the open fell. The wide track narrows to a peaty pathway as the three distinct cairns and trig point on the heathery summit are reached. This point on the Southern Upland Way provides a fine platform from which to savour the scenic delights of the Border Country.

CLOVENFORDS

38. CLOVENFORDS HOTEL - Clovenfords, Scottish Borders TD1 3LU. (01896) 850203 ***Colour Photo opposite p96***

Clovenfords clusters around the crossroads of the A72 and the B710; 3 miles (4.8km) west from Galashiels and 1 mile (1.6km) north of the River Tweed. Clovenfords Hotel is prominently positioned at the crossroads.

SITUATION *OS Map Landranger. Sheet 73 1:50,000 GR 449365*

The village was originally known as Whytbank Lea and only in later centuries as Clovenfords; the coaching inn and its nearby smithy, circa 1750s, have changed little with the passage of time. The turreted bow windows of the bar still remain, only Sir Walter Scott's statue and the electric light arriving in the twentieth century. The friendly wooden walled bar with its own entrance is well stocked and spacious with a strategically placed open fire. Solid tables, wall settles and bar stools line the extremities. By contrast the lounge bar is carpeted and comfortably warm with its central stone fireplace and tasteful rural prints and fading photographs decorating the wall. A comfortable dining room completes the ground floor facilities. In the original building, hazy sightings of one man and his dog (with a docked tail) have been seen passing through walls and moving furniture. No explanations are available.

OPEN:	Wednesday to Saturday, 11am-12 midnight Sunday to Tuesday, 11am-11pm
TYPE:	Free House
ON DRAUGHT:	Burton Ale, Caledonian 80/-, Dryborough Heavy, Alloa Light Ale, Guinness, Carlsberg Lager, Castlemain XXXX, Addlestone Cider
BOTTLED:	Selection of beers, stout, lager and cider
WHISKY:	Proprietary blends and 12 malts
WINE:	House white, dry and medium; red. Wine list of 22
FOOD:	Bar meals, lunch 12 noon-2pm, evening 6-9pm. Afternoon teas 4.30-6pm. Menu and specials blackboard
ACCOMMODATION:	2 double, 2 twin, all en-suite

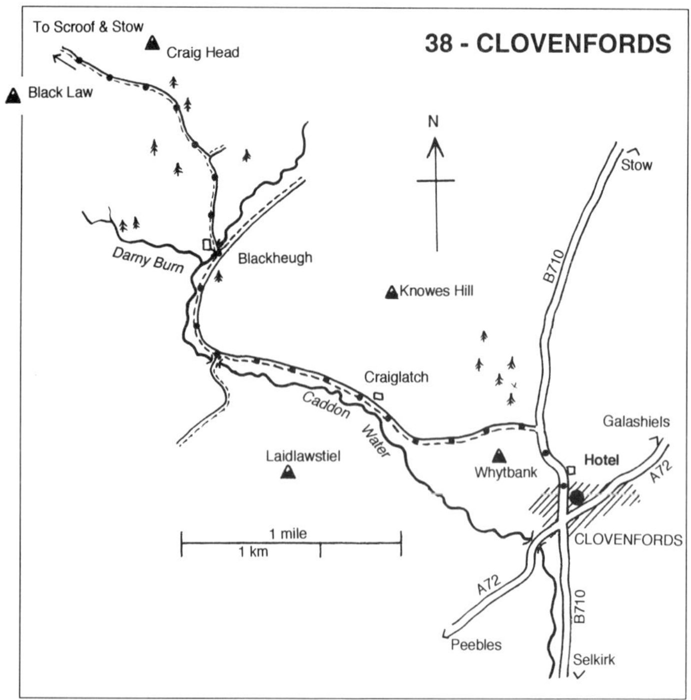

FACILITIES:	Beer garden, darts, dominoes, quiz machine, live folk festival one week in July
OPEN FIRES:	Bar, lounge bar and meeting room
WALKERS:	Welcome, dirty boots no problem in the bar - lino
CHILDREN:	Welcome, children's licence
DOGS:	Only in the bar
PARKING:	Park on the east side, walkers' cars left by arrangement

FOOD

An interesting and imaginative home-cooked menu, using local ingredients, with vegetarians, children and OAPs well catered for. Local favourites are steak and ale pie and grilled steak.

ITEMS OF LOCAL INTEREST

It was at Clovenfords Inn that Sir Walter Scott lodged prior to moving into nearby Ashiestiel; where he wrote *Marmion* and *The Lady of the Lake*. Wordsworth called in 1803, recorded in *Yarrow Revisited*, "And with the Tweed had travelled, And when we came to Clovenfords".

The inn closed in 1833, in all probability due to changing coach routes and the advent of the steam railway, reopening in 1901. Ten years later the statue of Sir Walter appeared; fashioned in 1910 by J.Archibald of Galashiels for a local parade, the frockcoat and trousers donated by a Gala' man. Unable to place the likeness in Gala' it was finally erected at the "Clovenfords", with an annuity of £100 for its annual upkeep.

WALKS

A fine scenic linear walk into the Moorfoot foothills, via Caddon Water to Stow; 10½ miles (17km), ascending 1073ft (327m). N from Clovenfords on the B710 for ½ mile, turn W over Whytebank col to Caddon Water at Blackhaugh. Continue N, passing Caddonhead to the isolated house of Scroof with its shelter of rowan and ash. Climb E with the burnside path to the cairned col N of Dunlee Hill and follow this path E through an L-shaped plantation descending with Back Burn to the Lodge and Lugate Farm. Beyond, a country lane leads N alongside Gala Water into Stow.

ETTRICKBRIDGE

39. CROSS KEYS INN - Ettrickbridge, Selkirk TD7 5JN. (01750) 452224

Ettrickbridge, a garden of a village, stands above and beside Ettrick Water on the B7009; 7½ miles (12km) south-west of the border town of Selkirk. The Cross Keys Inn is in the middle of the village on the north side of the road.

SITUATION *OS Map Landranger. Sheet 73 1:50,000 GR 388243*

A village local since the mid 1700s, this former coaching inn has always had the name Cross Keys Inn. A regular coach service operated from Selkirk to Tushielaw, with Ettrickbridge-end (as it was then known) the lynch pin of the operation. In 1928 the rough highway was tarmacked and in 1990 electric street lights shone in Ettrickbridge.

The exterior of the original building remains, with the stable section attached to the south end. The interior is much changed but the warm welcome still remains, as for those "gizened" travellers of yesteryear. An entrance porch, displaying local events, leads into a low oak-beamed bar, carpeted and cushioned with a welcoming log fire. The bright L-shaped counter is in character with the rural prints, local crafts (for sale), horse brasses and a baby's rocking chair. A pleasing decor providing a strong message, if any be needed, to wet and dirty walkers. The dining room is equally attractive and inviting. Self catering courtyard cottages, recently completed, to the rear.

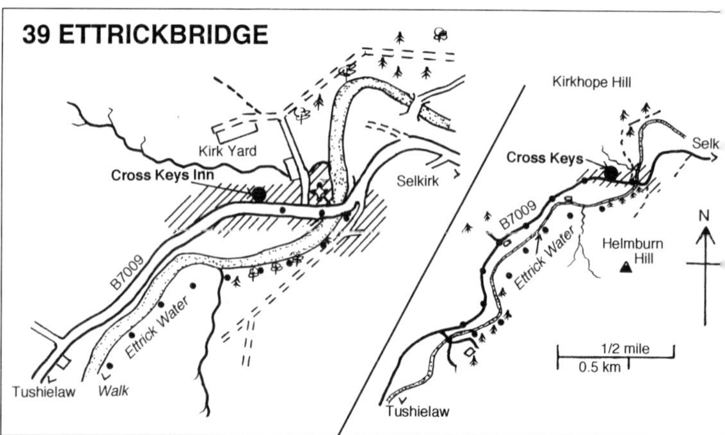

Ettrickbridge - Cross Keys Inn

OPEN:	Monday to Saturday, 12 noon-2.30pm, 6-11pm Sunday, 12.30-2.30pm, 6.30-11pm
TYPE:	Free House
ON DRAUGHT:	Caledonian Brewery 70/- Ale in the summer, Dryburghs Heavy, Alloa Light Ale, Carlsberg Export, Castlemain XXXX, Old English Dry Cider
BOTTLED:	Wee Heavy, beers, stout, lager and cider
WHISKY:	Proprietary blends and several malts
WINE:	House wine, white, medium; red. List, small but select
FOOD:	12 noon-1.45pm, 6-9pm in the bar and dining room. Menu with daily specials blackboard in the bar
ACCOMMODATION:	In the inn - 1 double, 1 twin, both en-suite. Courtyard cottages - 2 with 3 bedrooms, 3 with 2 bedrooms
FACILITIES:	Disabled facilities in bar toilets. Pool room, scrabble, dominoes, cards, quiz machine, bandit. Tennis, cricket and football pitches in the village
OPEN FIRES:	Iron stove in the bar, open fire in the dining room
WALKERS:	Welcome, please leave wet gear in the entrance porch
CHILDREN:	Welcome
DOGS:	No
PARKING:	Rear car park, cars can be left by arrangement

FOOD

The innovative menu is wisely on the small side, with local produce used wherever possible, from the inviting sandwich to succulent Border Aberdeen Angus steaks. A firm favourite with locals and visitors is locally cured home-cooked ham. Children and vegetarians catered for.

ITEMS OF LOCAL INTEREST

ride by Ettrick's stream,
'Mang bonnie trees wi' tints agleam,
The Brig-end pules, yon fishers dream.

Anon

The Ettrick Valley has its share of the occult: "The Jingler's Room" at Oakwood Tower, "The Grey Lady" at Singlie House plus tales of Michael Scott the Wizard. In the 1890s a thriving Draughts Club held meetings at Cherrydean, Ettrickbridge.

WALKS

A circular riverside walk of tranquil beauty, 3 miles (4.8km), best seen in spring or autumn. N through the village to the brig bearing "Scott of Hardens" crest, cross and turn right into the trees above Ettrick Water. 1/2 mile (0.8km) beyond, by a feeder burn, leave the trees to cross the burn over four strapped larch poles. Continue SW by the waterside (careful on the slippery stones), eventually ascending via a wall end to three grassy knowes leading to the dark conifers. A distinct path winds for 100yds through the trees to the water's edge, where a thin overgrown trod continues W with the river to Pine Lodge and a bridge, circa 1891. Cross and turn right onto the road to Ettrickbridge.

LANGHOLM

40. BUCK HOTEL - High Sreet, Langholm, Dumfriesshire DG13 0JH. (01387) 380400

Langholm, the "Muckle Toon" at the confluence of Esk and Ewe Waters and the junction of the A7, B709 and B7068, sits 20 miles (32km) north of Carlisle and 26 miles (41.6km) south-west of Hawick. The Buck Hotel is in the vicinity of the Townhead Bridge.

SITUATION *OS Map Landranger. Sheet 79 1:50,000 GR 364847*

The approaches to Langholm, once described as "the most beautiful of all between Edinburgh and London", herald a small mill town of singular

Langholm - Buck Hotel

character. Severe at first glance, warm and welcoming on full acquaintance; as is The Buck Hotel. A coaching inn whose title deeds go back to 1728 and whose out-houses included a brew-house and quartered ostlers, horses and 'smiths. In the 1939-45 conflict, it housed the SS commando who fearlessly raided the Lofoeton Islands and St Nazaire.

The bar side door and the front door into the mosaic floored entrance hall open directly from the High Street, into a cocoon of fine pitch-pine, including the ceilings in the bar, front-snug, lounge and stair case. The welcoming bar, with its full-length counter, shining taps, glasses and bottles, confirms its "best local in town" tag; whilst the snug gives that cosy quiet room feel. A pub to rest content in.

An' ken that in the Buck and Croon Hotels
They'd launch my tale to scorn, altho' gudsake.

MacDiarmid

OPEN:	Monday to Wednesday, 11am-2.30pm, 5-11pm
	Thursday to Saturday, 11am-2.30pm, 5-12 midnight
	Sunday, 12.30-2.30pm, 6.30-11pm
TYPE:	Free House
ON DRAUGHT:	McEwan's 70/-, Theakston BB, Younger's PA, Maclay PA, Guinness, Heineken Lager, McEwan's Lager, Strongbow

BOTTLED:	A full selection of beers, stout, lager and cider
WHISKY:	Proprietary blends, 2 malts. Langholm's spirit is gin
WINE:	House - white, dry and sweet; red
FOOD:	Lunch 12 noon-2pm, evening supper
ACCOMMODATION:	4 double, 1 single with shared facilities
FACILITIES:	Pool room with darts, dominoes. Courtyard beer garden
OPEN FIRES:	No, gas fires in the bar and snug
WALKERS:	Welcome, parties/groups wishing food please advise
CHILDREN:	Not allowed in the bar
DOGS:	Obedient dogs
PARKING:	Limited space in rear yard

FOOD

A menu of well cooked dishes, in the best country tradition. Evening groups up to 46 can be catered for.

ITEMS OF LOCAL INTEREST

Langholm stands on the battle site of Arkinholme (Langholm's old name), where the Douglas family was crushed in 1455.

Langholm celebrates its colourful Fair and Common Riding on the last Friday of July, when the proclamation at the "Crying of the Fair" declares that disturbers of the peace "shall sit down on their bare knees and pray seven times for the King, and thrice for the Muckle Laird o' Ralton", the "Laird" being the illegitimate son of Charles II.

Birthplace and burial place of Hugh MacDiarmid, pen name of Christopher Murray Grieve, acclaimed as one of Scotland's greatest poets.

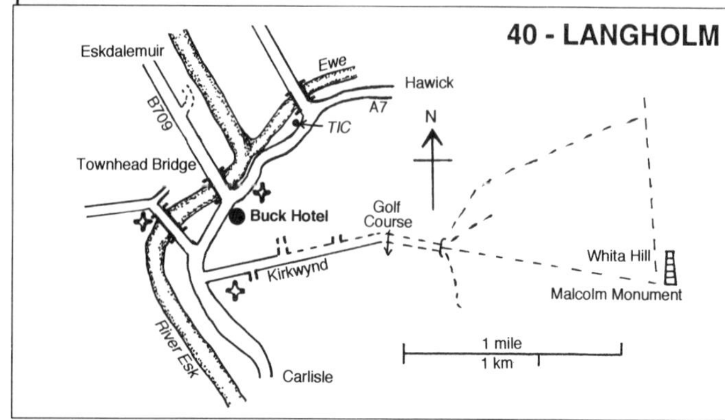

WALKS

A 2 mile (3.2km) return journey, ascending heather-clad Whita Hill to the Malcolm memorial. S from the Buck to the square ascend the steep Kirkwynd (a rail is at hand to assist), continuing E past the golf course to a stile and a choice of paths. Take the centre one and go straight on up, E to the giant obelisk of Langholm stone, erected in 1835 to Sir John Malcolm, one of the four "Knights of Eskdale". Whita Hill provides panoramic views, the Lakes across the glistening Solway, distant Criffel, the heights of Eskdale and Liddesdale. Return by descending N for 600yds then sharp left to meet the outward path from Langholm.

Walks around Langholm and Byreburn Wood by Buccleuch Estates are available from the Tourist Information Centre.

INNERLEITHEN

41. TRAQUAIR ARMS HOTEL - Traquair Road, Innerleithen, Peeblesshire EH44 6PD. (01896) 830229. Fax (01896) 830260

Innerleithen stands on the junction of the A72 and B709, by Traquair Water and the River Tweed; 6 1/2 miles (10.4km) east of Peebles. The Traquair Arms is on the B709 Traquair road, 100yds south of the High Street.

Innerleithen - Traquair Arms Hotel

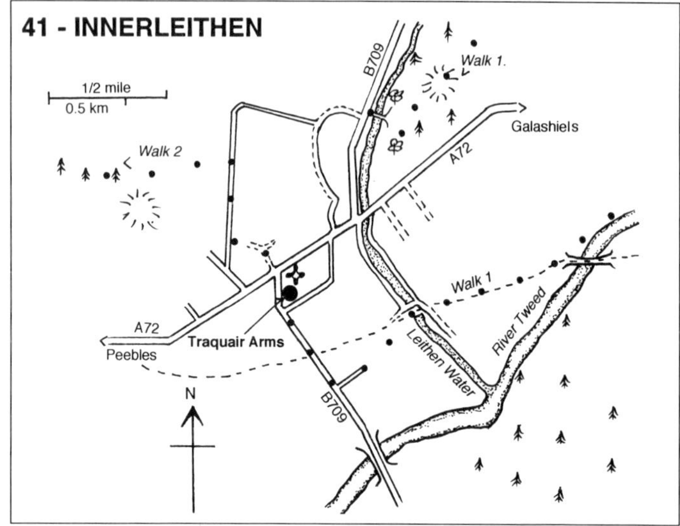

SITUATION *OS Map Landranger. Sheet 73 1:50,000 GR 330365*

Close to the town centre, yet out of earshot, the stone built one time coaching inn of "Riddells", circa 1836, is now known as the Traquair Arms. This traditional, friendly, family-run hotel was enlarged in the early 1900s, with the addition of an east wing. The high ceilinged lounge bar, left from the entrance hall, is comfortable with chintzy chairs and stools, buttoned velvet wall settees and a scattering of tables. It is a bar of rural prints and shiny bottles, polished wood and a fine log fire, where space and company go hand in hand, before leading to the hotel garden, or the Pirn lounge dining room. The restaurant is tastefully laid and log fired.

The Traquair Arms has a benign spirit, a rare phenomenon in Border inns, with hair piled high and a long grey dress complete with bustle. Seen only from the back view and only in the original building, this "Grey Lady of Riddell's" remains a mystery.

OPEN:	All year, 11am-11pm (Christmas/New Year excepted)
TYPE:	Free House
ON DRAUGHT:	Traquair Bear Ale, Greenmantle Ale, Broughton Ale, McEwan's Tartan Special, McEwan's Pale Ale, Carlsberg Lager, Addlestones Cider
BOTTLED:	Greenmantle Export, Traquair House Ale, Caledonian 80/- & 70/-, Broughton Oatmeal Stout, plus standard choices

WHISKY:	Proprietary blends and carefully considered malts
WINE:	House white, dry and medium; red. The wine list of 37, with 4 from Scotland, provides a good read and a fine glass
FOOD:	Daily - bar meals, 12 noon-9pm; dinner, 7-9pm dining room; afternoon and high tea, 2.30-5.30pm. Varied menus
ACCOMMODATION:	3 double, 2 twin, 2 family and 3 single; all en-suite
FACILITIES:	A salmon stretch on the Tweed, drying room, garden tables. Trestle table at front entrance
OPEN FIRES:	Log burning in the bar and dining room
WALKERS:	Most welcome, route details provided by Traquair Arms
CHILDREN:	Welcome
DOGS:	Welcome, dog dishes and towels provided
PARKING:	Private parking at the side/rear. Walkers may leave cars, plus route details, by arrangement

FOOD
With the exception of ice cream every dish is prepared in the kitchen from fresh local produce, providing the base for imaginative menus of regional dishes. Particular favourites are cullen skink, Finnan savoury, Traquair steak pie, pheasant in green apple, bread and butter pud.

ITEMS OF LOCAL INTEREST
Traquair House, a royal residence from the twelfth to the sixteenth centuries, is open to the public. Its famous Bear Gates, the subject of much discussion, give their name to a beer brewed in the grounds. St Ronan's Well, a medicinal spa made famous by the Waverley novels of Sir Walter Scott, lies north of Innerleithen. Visit also the water-powered printing works.

WALKS
1) Fell and forest, 9 miles (14.4km), 1460ft (445m) ascent, E by Tweedside to Walkerburn. Cross the main road to the farm track by Walker Burn. N for $1^1/_2$ miles (2.4km) to the isolated ruin of Priesthope, continue N then follow the left fork of the burn NW. The broad track then ascends right and is abandoned at this point. Continue with the burn and a thin path for 250yds before climbing W to the bealach of heathery Priesthope Hill and grassy Glede Knowe. Now begins a fine Border ridge walk S; ascend the steep summit of Priesthope then follow the wall/fence to Kirnie Law, note the astonishing concrete reservoir.

Descend S from Kirnie Law on a track through the trees which opens to provide fine views of Innerleithen, the Tweed Valley and the

Tweedsmuir Hills. Continue SW, via an ancient fort, to Cuddy Bridge, Innerleithen.

2) By forest, fields and Tweed via the TV mast to Glenormiston Farm, then left across the A72 to cottages and Tweedside. Follow the riverbank andthe old railway to Tweed Bridge and Innerleithen.

MOUNTBENGER

42. GORDON ARMS HOTEL-Mountbenger, Yarrow Valley, Selkirkshire TD7 5LE. (01750) 824232 or 824222 ***Colour photo see cover***
At the intersection of the A708 and B709. 13 miles (20.8km) west of Selkirk and 22 miles (35.2km) east of Moffat; 9 miles (14.4km) south of Innerleithen, 22 miles (35.5km) north-west of Hawick. The inn stands in the north west quadrant of the crossroads.

SITUATION *OS Map Landranger. Sheet 73 1:50,000 GR 308249*
The inn was built by John Gordon (hence the name), a contractor to the Duke of Buccleuch in the early 1800s. A licence application of 21st May 1828, supported by James Hogg, the "Ettrick Shepherd", is on show in the bar; "John Gordon has always behaved civilly and honourably to his customers".

Prominently situated by the crossroads in upper Yarrow, the rough-cast walls of the Gordon Arms are easily seen. Cosy, clean and comfortable, with the hand of border hospitality evident in both bars, sheep and rugby memorabilia predominate and comfy old chairs hug the fireside. Constant "crack" of fishing and sheep, ways and wayfarers is accompanied by mine host's unrecognisable tunes. A resident's lounge and pleasant dining room complete the ground floor of this family-run inn, where walkers and those who love the Borders are most welcome.

Our very hearts blood has set off with a run
At thought of a sight of the Gordon!

Anon

OPEN:	Summer (Easter to mid October) & winter weekends 11am-11pm Winter weekdays 11am-2.30pm, 7-11pm
TYPE:	Free House
ON DRAUGHT:	Greenmantle Ale, Tennent's 70/-, Broughton Oatmeal Stout, Tennent's Special, Light Ale & Lager. Dry Blackthorn Cider
BOTTLED:	Broughton Old Jock, Broughton Old Stout, Guinness, Carlsberg Special Brew plus standards
WHISKY:	Proprietary blends and 56 carefully selected malts

St Mary's Loch - Tibbie Shiels Inn
Moffat - Black Bull Hotel

Seahouses - The Olde Ship Hotel
Gifford - Goblin Ha' Hotel

WINE:	House white, dry and medium; red
FOOD:	Daily specials - blackboard, plus menus. Lunch 12 noon-2.30pm; high teas (summer) 4-6pm; evening 7-9pm
ACCOMMODATION:	Bedrooms - 3 twin, 2 double, 1 family; 1 bath/toilet per 3 rooms. Bunkhouse - 20 bunks with shared showers etc.
FACILITIES:	Bunkhouse drying room & pool room. Walkers' pick-up service ex Southern Upland Way (SUW) - 6 mile radius. Accordion & Fiddle Club. Local guidebooks for sale
OPEN FIRES:	In the bar, lounge bar and resident's lounge
WALKERS:	Very welcome, as the sign says
CHILDREN:	Welcome, not allowed in the bar
DOGS:	Welcome, three Old English sheepdogs are residents
PARKING:	Hotel parking with a field overflow. Walkers' cars left by arrangement, leave details of route plan

FOOD

Home-cooked from local produce, favourites being Yarrow lamb chops and grilled trout from Yarrow fisheries. Helpings are on the generous side. Vegetarian meals and children's helpings are available.

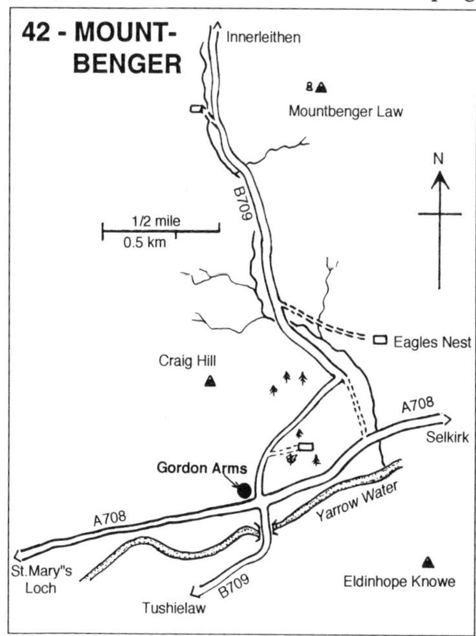

ITEMS OF LOCAL INTEREST

The solitude of the green billowing hills that surround the Gordon Arms drew the literati of the 1800s to join the Border's own genius at Mountbenger. Sir Walter Scott, "Christopher North", Allan Cunningham and William Wordsworth all bided awhile; it was at the Gordon Arms that

Scott and Hogg finally parted in 1830. "I cannot tell what it was, but there was something in his manner that distressed me", wrote the shepherd.

WALKS

An ascent of the twin tops of Mountbenger Law; wind N from the Gordon Arms, via the B709 to Mountbengerhope cottage past Mountbenger (site of Hogg's Farm). Turn E onto a track then N ascending the open fell via the corrie rim to the main cairned summit. Return S via the central ridge to the lower top for a fine panorama of the water of Yarrow. Continue the descent S on the grassy slopes to join the track, from the Eagles Nest, by the B709. Return S to the Gordon Arms.

Many fine walks are within a 6 mile radius of the Gordon Arms; hotel and bunkhouse guests can avail themselves of the courtesy bus.

TUSHIELAW

43. TUSHIELAW INN - Ettrick Valley, Selkirkshire, Borders TD7 5HT. (01750) 462205 ***Colour photo opposite p96***

Gathered around the offset junction of the B709, B7009 and B711 is the inn, the hill, the farm and the pele of Tushielaw; 14$^1/_2$ miles (23.2km) south-west of Selkirk and 16 miles (25.6km) west of Hawick.

SITUATION *OS Map Landranger. Sheet 79 1:50,000 GR 303177*

Beneath the flanks of Tushie Law (spelt Tusshyla circa 1500) and above the water of Ettrick stands Tushielaw Inn, an old toll house and coaching inn. Thomson's map of 1824 marked a major drove road from Peebles to Hawick via Tushielaw, an ideal site for a toll bar. Later it developed as a coaching inn, servicing the run from Selkirk and providing a "stop" on the horse-drawn tours of the early 1900s.

The original flat frontage was improved with the addition of dormer windows and an arched porch, though it still presents a somewhat severe exterior. Not so the interior, which is greatly enhanced by the friendly welcome and the generous helpings. A front hall with Victorian bells (tap-room, parlour etc.) and an old "Scottish AA" sign advising the motorist to "Gang Warily" leads into a small cosy carpeted bar with a background whisper of fine music, a regal brass till and walls peppered with the past. A larger lounge bar adjoins, overlooking the Ettrick.

Begone the thocht o' Wunter's cauld,
Begone the thocht I'm gettin auld,
Begone thin bluid and heid now bauld -
I'm gaun tae Tushie! John Dodds

OPEN:	Summer, 12 noon-2.30pm, 6-11pm, Sunday, 12.30-11pm. Winter, 12 noon-2.30pm, 7-11pm, Sunday, 12.30-11pm. Closed Monday and Tuesday
TYPE:	Free House
ON DRAUGHT:	Broughton Ale, McEwan's Pale Ale, Tennent's Lager
BOTTLED:	Newcastle Brown Ale, Greenmantle Extra, McEwan's 80/-, Belhaven Export, Carslberg Special Brew, stouts, cider
WHISKY:	Proprietary blends plus single and blended malts
WINE:	House white, dry and medium; red. A small thoughtful list
FOOD:	Lunch 12.30-2pm, supper 6-9pm. Daily specials on quaint blackboards, menus. Takeaway meals available
ACCOMMODATION:	1 double en-suite, 1 double, 1 twin shared bathroom
FACILITIES:	Disabled persons' toilet, drying room, beer garden, pick-up service for Southern Upland Way (SUW), free trout loch fishing. Darts
OPEN FIRES:	Two iron Victorian fireplaces in the bar and restaurant
WALKERS:	Welcome, along with cyclists, fishers, shooters, etc.
CHILDREN:	Welcome, not allowed in the bar
DOGS:	No
PARKING:	Limited to the roadside

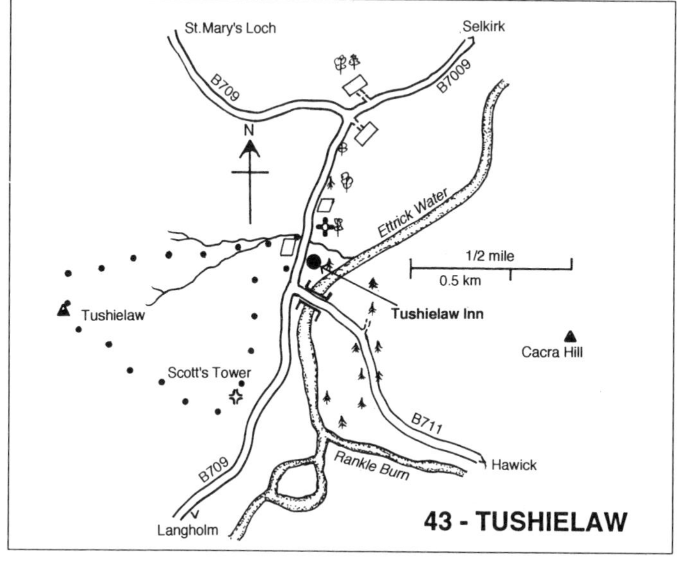

FOOD

The imaginative bar menu and daily specials will tempt, but not prepare, the traveller for the quality or the quantity of the chosen dish, be it a filled baguette, local trout, pheasant or venison. Sunday afternoon teas in summer and a complete à la carte menu for the dining room.

ITEMS OF LOCAL INTEREST

The scenery and the solitude of Ettrick. The valley was home to James Hogg, the Ettrick shepherd, who "taught the wandering winds to sing"; and to Boston of Ettrick, a charismatic "fire and brimstone" preacher. Adam Scott of Tushielaw (a renowned local Reiver) was hanged by James V for his nocturnal deeds. A mile or two up the Rankle Burn, Clear Burn surges through Buck Cleuch, the birthplace of the family of Buccleuch.

WALKS

A 2 mile (3.2km) circular walk to the haunted tower of Tushielaw, ascending 712ft (217m) to the summit of Tushie Law.

Opposite the inn a stile leads uphill to a "water tank", above which a distinct sheep track contours left for 600yds to the ruins of Tushielaw tower. This powerful pele did not save Adam Scott from the hangman's rope, a fate he had bestowed on many others, as the grooves in the surrounding branches verify.

Continue to the grassy SE shoulder, join a twin track ascending W to the rounded summit of Tushie Law. The view of Ettrick and the horseshoe of surrounding hills delights the eye. Descend E and then NE, on the twin track by Small Burn, for the final mile to Syke Cottage and Tushie.

PEEBLES

44. GLENTRESS HOTEL & TRAVELODGE - Kirnlaw, Peebles EH45 8NB. Tel & Fax (01721) 720100 ***Colour photo opposite p97***

$2^{1}/_{2}$ miles (4km) east from Peebles on the A72 at the entrance to Glentress Forest. The Glentress Hotel stands on the east side of the forest drive above the River Tweed.

SITUATION *OS Map Landranger. Sheet 73 1:50,000 GR 284396*
Strategically situated for the walker, on the fringes of Glentress Forest and the Moorfoot Hills to the north, with Cardrona forest and the Manor Hills to the

south. Built in 1958, in the style of the time, the Travelodge may appear slighty incongruous; a fear soon repelled by the friendly welcome and good service in the much improved interior that accentuates the panorama to the south. The partitioned spacious eating area (80 seats) leads to a small coffee lounge and the bar. A carpeted bar of cushioned wall seats in open alcoves, where mine host is happy to cater for walkers (with wiped boots). The hotel's courtesy bus, by arrangement, removes the problems of linear walks.

OPEN:	All year 11am-11pm
TYPE:	Free House
ON DRAUGHT:	Alloa Export 80/- Ale, Alloa Special 70/-, Carlsberg Lager, Gaymer's Old English Cider
BOTTLED:	A selection of beers, stout, lager and cider
WHISKY:	Proprietary blends and several malts
WINE:	House white, dry and medium; red. A worldwide wine list of 35
FOOD:	Breakfast 8-10am; lunch 12 noon-2.30pm; afternoon & high teas 3-6pm; supper 6-9pm (w/e 9.30pm). Menu and blackboard
ACCOMMODATION:	14 double/twin, all en-suite
FACILITIES:	For disabled persons, courtesy mini-bus, beer garden
OPEN FIRES:	No
WALKERS:	Most Welcome
CHILDREN:	Welcome
DOGS:	Not in the eating areas
PARKING:	Two parks, walkers' cars left with management's approval. Route plans to be left for adventurous walks

FOOD
A full and changing menu of home-cooked dishes, using local produce such as trout and salmon when in season. The steak pie will satisfy the hungriest of walkers. Children and vegetarians catered for.

ITEMS OF LOCAL INTEREST
Glentress is the oldest forest in southern Scotland, dating from 1920, and as such has settled down to provide a rich mix of habitat for the indigenous flora and fauna.

Nearby Peebles is a place to wander in and soak up the past; the civic Beltane Week, Agricultural Show, "Highland" Games, Arts Festival and Tweeddale Museum are colourful and attractive.

WALKS
A choice of variable, well waymarked circular forest walks, from either

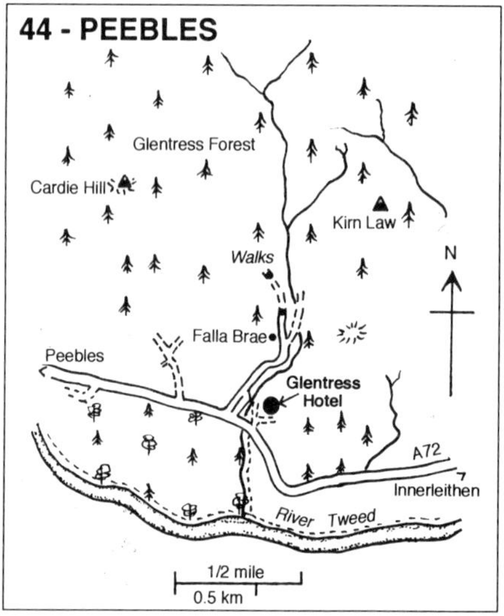

Glentress Hotel or Forest Enterprise Falla Brae car park and information centre. Maps and route details available from the Hotel or FE.

A stroll around the lochans and picnic areas above Falla Brae.

Cardie Hill - $2\frac{1}{4}$ miles (3.6km) in $1\frac{1}{4}$ hours.

Kirn Law Walk - 3 miles (4.8km) in $1\frac{3}{4}$ hours.

Caresman Hill - $4\frac{1}{2}$ miles (7.2km) in $2\frac{3}{4}$ hours.

Glentress Circuit - $5\frac{3}{4}$ miles (9.2km) in 4 hours.

Over forest roads and paths, identified by colour coded waymarks, routes that are rich in interest, wildlife and fine views of upper Tweeddale.

45. KINGSMUIR HOTEL - Springhill Road, Peebles, Borders EH45 9EP. (01721) 720151. Fax (01721) 721795

Peebles is 23 miles (36.8km) south of Edinburgh via the A703 and 19miles (30.4km) west from Galashiels. The Kingsmuir Hotel is south of the Tweed via the Tweed Bridge; once across continue south along Springhill Road for 400yds.

SITUATION *OS Map Landranger. Sheet 73 1:50,000 GR 253398*

Peebles, an interesting and ancient town, founded in 1261, graces both banks of the silvery Tweed and has from the earliest times been a favourite residence for Scottish royal families. Place names such as Kings Muir suggest regal connections.

Built in the mid 1800s as a mill-owner's residence and later used as a hunting lodge, the Kingsmuir was converted to a country house hotel in the 1950s, later to become today's family-run hotel under the present owners. Solid and locally styled with windows on every side to maximise light and views, this comfortable haven provides a welcome for all who love the great outdoors. The

Peebles - Kingsmuir Hotel

spacious bar is divided into three sections - a friendly bar supported by southbank locals and visitors. The lounge, dining room and sun-lounge, with walls tastefully decorated with rural and historical prints, are very informal but far too well furnished to enter in mountain gear. Considerable distances have been traversed to sample the Kingsmuir's cooking.

OPEN:	All year, 11am-11pm (12 midnight Friday and Saturday)
TYPE:	Free House
ON DRAUGHT:	Broughton Greenmantle Ale, Broughton Light, Tartan Special, Carlsberg Hof, Tennent's Lager, Taunton Cider
BOTTLED:	A selection of beers, stout, lager and cider
WHISKY:	Proprietary blends, plus 20 or so customer's choice malts
WINE:	House white, dry/medium; red. A small interesting list
FOOD:	Bar - lunch 12 noon-2pm, supper 7-9.30pm Dining room - lunch 12 noon-2pm, dinner 7-9pm
ACCOMMODATION:	3 double, 4 twin, 1 family, 2 single - all en-suite
FACILITIES:	Garden tables, seats and sun-shades. Drying room
OPEN FIRES:	Coal fire in the Lounge
WALKERS:	Most welcome
CHILDREN:	Welcome
DOGS:	Welcome
PARKING:	At the front, cars may be left by arrangement

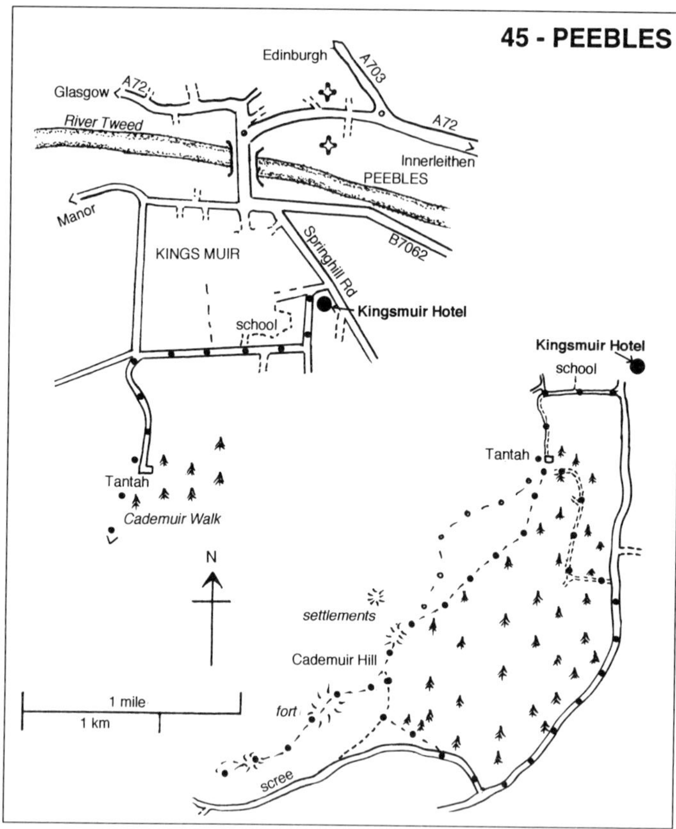

FOOD

Traditional Scottish home cooking, using fresh produce in season (no frozen vegetables or meat) and Grannie's recipes. Dishes such as cullen skink, Kingsmuir steak pie, Tweed kettle of salmon, apple pie and cheesecake are very popular.

ITEMS OF LOCAL INTEREST

The Beltane Festivities of Peebles are held annually, when on the 2nd of May the Beltane Queen is selected. Many centuries ago fires on the surrounding hills honoured the deity Baal, Beltane signifying the fire of

Baal. Sports such as archery and horse racing remain today.
At Beltane, when ilk bodie bownis (everybody makes ready to go)
To Peblis to the Play,

The restored tower of Neidpath and Cademuir Hill are worth a visit.

WALKS

From Kingsmuir to Cademuir (the Great Battle) Hill, the scene of King Arthur's seventh battle against the Pagan; 6 miles (9.6km) ascending 1007ft (307m). From Kingsmuir into Springwood Road and Bonnington Road (signposted Cademuir), then Craigerne Lane by Peebles High School. Left at Cademuir International School to the entrance of Tantah house, then right onto a bridlepath and the open fell. Ascend SW, on a grassy track to Cademuir Plantation. From the corner of the conifers turn and marvel at the scenery N, before crossing the grassy ridge to Cademuir summit.

Descend SSW to the central col then ascend to the stone ringed summit of Cademuir Hill, a fine Cromlech known as "Arthur's Oven" stood here until the early 1800s. Ahead, to the SW, the hogs-back ridge is peppered with pre-historic forts and settlements and distant views demand attention. For the return, descend NE to the col.

1) Descend S alongside the wall to reach the road below, turn left, (S) then NE and N for 1$^{3}/_{4}$ miles (2.8km) to a forest road on the left. Follow this road contouring N and NW through the trees to the stile at Tantah.

2) Walk N below the ridge to a lower col, descending NE to Tantah.

For a riverside walk, Peebles via Neidpath Tower and Manor Bridge to Lyne Station - see *A Tweed Walk* by Borders Regional Council, from the TIC.

ESKDALEMUIR

46. HART MANOR HOTEL - Eskdalemuir, Nr Langholm, Dumfriesshire G13 0QQ. Tel & Fax (01387) 373217 *Colour photo opposite p97*

Eskdalemuir, in the winding valley of the White Esk, sits astride the junction of the B709 and B723; 12 miles (19.2km) north-west of Langholm and 14 miles (22.4km) north-east of Lockerbie. Hart Manor Hotel stands above the Esk, 1 mile south of the village.

SITUATION *OS Map Landranger. Sheet 79 1:50,000 GR 252978*
Hart Manor, high in picturesque Eskdale, was originally a seventeenth-century cottage known as Rennaldburn, extended to Hart Manor in 1845, a

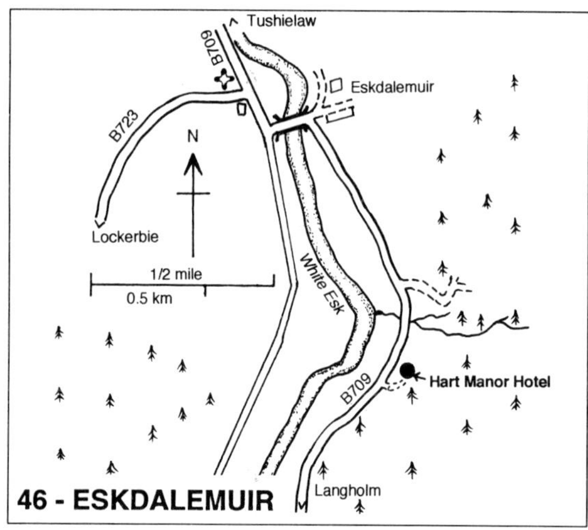

shooting lodge on the Buccleuch estates. In 1904 the lodge was sold for a doctor's residence, later to change hands in 1976 to be converted into a pub. In 1979 it was elevated to an hotel. The rather serious exterior of Hart Manor (its nearest "competitor" is at least 10 miles/16km away) is soon displaced by the genuinely warm welcome and the well kept ale. Two bars, front and back, are comfortable, "pubby" places in which to relax, a pleasing mix of ancient and modern, locals and visitors. The atmosphere is personified by a Lomax print of a Georgian duel, "For he had spoken lightly of a women's name". Sitting room and dining room, though small, are in keeping with the gentle comfort of the place. Visit the kitchen to savour the panorama of Eskdale and Ettrick Pen.

OPEN:	Spring, summer, autumn,	12 noon-2.30pm, 6.30-11pm
	Winter (November-Easter),	closed Tuesdays
TYPE:	Free House	
ON DRAUGHT:	Greenmantle Special Bitter, McEwan's 70/-, Murphy's Irish Stout, Carlsberg Export Hof, Strongbow Dry Cider	
BOTTLED:	A range of beers, stout, lager and cider	
WHISKY:	Proprietary blends, plus de-luxe and 28/30 single malts	
WINE:	House white, dry Bordeaux/medium Mosel; red, claret. A considered and reasonably priced wine list	
FOOD:	Bar menu, includes daily specials, 12.30-2pm, 6.30-9.30pm. Dinner menu 7.30-8pm in the dining room	
ACCOMMODATION:	5 twin en-suite, 2 double sharing bathroom	

FACILITIES:	Drying room. In the bar - darts, dominoes and chess
OPEN FIRES:	In the front bar, back bar, resident's sitting room
WALKERS:	Most welcome, muddy and wet gear in the vestibule please
CHILDREN:	Welcome, 8.30pm is Cinderella time in the bars
DOGS:	Very welcome
PARKING:	Hotel car parks, walker's cars left with proprietor's consent; please leave route plan

FOOD

All the meals are prepared from fresh local produce when in season, nothing frozen, fish all wild, and cooked by mine host. Specialising in local venison, grouse, duck, Border lamb, Aberdeen Angus beef plus puddings; steaks and traditional Sunday roasts are particular favourites.

ITEMS OF LOCAL INTEREST

3 miles (4.8km) south on the summit of Shaw Rig Hill is the grave of King Shaw, a Pictish monarch. Close by is the "Diel's Jingle", site of an ancient fair where "Hand-Fasting or Hand-in-Fist" was solemnised (a custom from Roman times). Unmarried persons could choose a partner and live with the chosen one for one year. If all was sweetness marriage took place, if sourness marred the year the couple separated. In later years a priest from Melrose Abbey confirmed marriages made by Hand-Fasting; the priest's name was "John Buik-a-Bosom"!

Eskdalemuir hosts the largest Bhuddist Monastery outside Tibet, plus an Observatory and Seismology Station. Above Benpath, by Westkirk School, stands the Thomas Telford Memorial 1757-1834.

WALKS

A fine hike of 6 miles (9.6km) over the breezy fells above Eskdalemuir, E of the village via the farm track N below Clerk Hill to the Roman fort at Reaburnfoot. The track swings NNE on an old Roman road with the Rae Burn, over open country below Wisp Hill Rig to Raeburnside and Mid Raeburn. Ascend E with the bridlepath over open fell to Grey Hill at the forest's edge; or alternatively at the rig top prior to Grey Hill, SW over Wisp Hill and Clerk Hill. Descend SW from Grey Hill, with the path, to join a farm track at Windshiel Grain leading to Eskdalemuir.

ST MARY'S LOCH

47. TIBBIE SHIELS INN - St Mary's Loch, Selkirkshire TD7 5LH. (01750) 442231 ***Colour photo opposite p128***
On the narrow isthmus between St Mary's Loch and Loch of the Lowes, Tibbie's nestles close by the A708 road; 18 miles (28.8km) south west of Selkirk and 15½ miles (24.8km) north-east of Moffat.

SITUATION *OS Map Landranger. Sheet 79 1:50,000 GR 241205*
Born in Ettrick in 1782, Isabella (Tibbie) Shiel moved into St Mary's cottage when widowed in 1824. This spirited women transformed the cottage into a welcoming haven for wayfarers, and her spirit lives on: "Folk a' ken me best as Tibbie Shiels and I dar'say when I'm deid and gone this place will still be ca'ed Tibbie Shiels's".

Subsequent additions have not enhanced the external appeal of the building, for today it is somewhat of a white-washed stone and timber hotch-potch, internally it remains welcoming and full of memories. The bar room, with old photographs (one of Tibbie plus ghost), is small (although 13 people slept there in Tibbie's day!), the bar counter is but "five persons wide" and the ceiling low. Like as not the door lintel will split your skull if you stand 5ft 10in: "Duck or Grouse" says the notice. Yet regulars would have it no other way. Turn right on entering, by the "Walkers Welcome" sign, for Tibbie's Kitchen, a room of character and authenticity. The annexe, circa 1930, on the north gable is now the dining room. Tibbie's is a popular overnight stop on the SUW and a favoured watering-hole for thirsty walkers.

OPEN: *Summer:*
Monday to Thursday, 11am-11pm
Friday and Saturday, 11am-12 midnight
Closed all day Sunday 12.30-11pm
Winter (November to Easter):
As summer except Monday

TYPE: Free House

ON DRAUGHT: Greenmantle Ale, Belhaven 80/- Ale, Belhaven Best, Carlsberg Lager

BOTTLED: Newcastle Brown, Old Jock, Carlsberg Special, Special Vat, plus selection of beer, stout, lager and cider

WHISKY: Standard blends, plus 50 selected and varied malts

WINE: House white, dry/medium; red. A surprising wine list

FOOD: Bar meals during opening hours. Afternoon/high teas in Tibbie's Kitchen. Evening, à la carte in the dining room. Menus and a daily specials blackboard

ACCOMMODATION: 4 double, 1 family all en-suite

FACILITIES: Camping/caravan area (plans to extend), free fishing to residents;

	walking guides, local interest, OS maps for sale. Darts, dominoes, cribbage and piped music
OPEN FIRES:	Stove in the bar, fire in Tibbie's Kitchen
WALKERS:	Most welcome
CHILDREN:	Welcome, bar has children's licence
DOGS:	No, only Guide Dogs
PARKING:	Inn park, walkers' cars and route left by arrangement

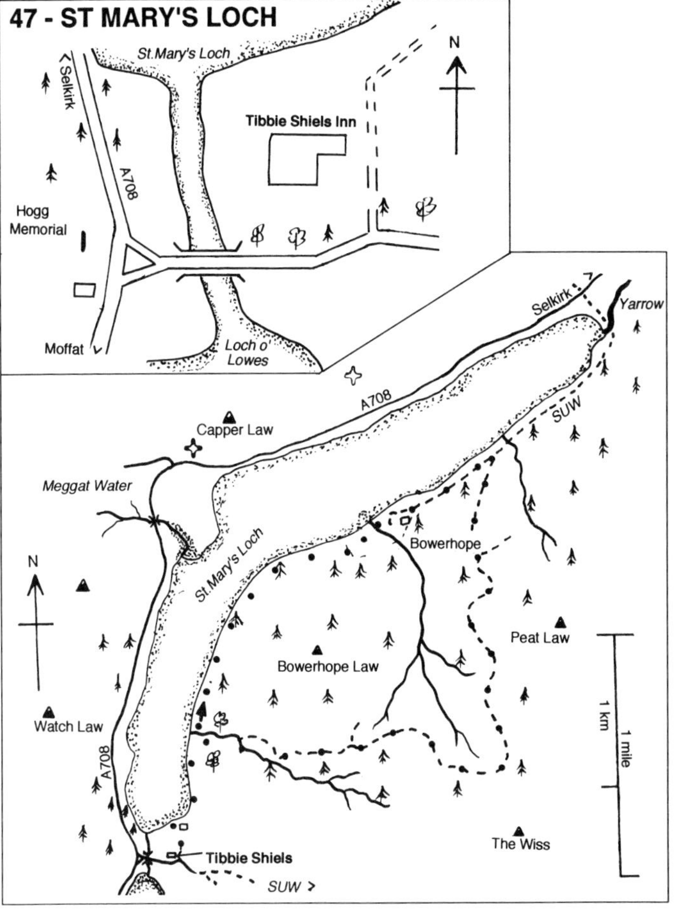

FOOD
Waitress served, a wide range of choice, from tasty local trout to a hot "Holy Mole" chilli from Peru (no connection with Tibbie's mole-catching husband). The home-made cloutie dumpling is a must for energetic walkers.

ITEMS OF INTEREST
Tibbie's was much favoured by the literary giants of the past including Scott, Hogg, North, publisher Robert Chambers (who included Tibbie's in *The Picture of Scotland*), Robert L.Stevenson, Carlyle and Stoddart, the angling poet. St Mary's Loch, immortalised by Wordsworth's *"The swan on still St Mary's lake floats double, swan and shadow"*, provides sailing, windsurfing, fishing and lochside walks.

WALKS
Too numerous to detail, but not to be missed, are St Marys Loch and Loch of the Lowes, St Mary's Kirk Yard, the spectacular waterfalls of the Grey Mares Tail and Dobs Linn and the dark mysterious Loch Skeen with its surrounding summits. Four walks from Tibbie's and nine, within a short drive, are included in *The Border Country - A Walker's Guide* by Alan Hall. The Southern Upland Way passes by and provides a picturesque route.

TWEEDSMUIR

48. THE CROOK INN - Tweedsmuir, Peeblesshire ML12 6QN. (018997) 272
1 mile (1.6km) north of Tweedsmuir village, the Crook Inn stands alone by the scenic A701 road and the silvery Tweed; 18 miles (28.8km) south of Peebles and 17 miles (27.2km) north of Moffat.

SITUATION *OS Map Landranger. Sheet 72 1:50,000 GR 111264*
A haven since the ninth century, its name comes from the Norse word "Crook" - a bend in the river. A cattle drovers' rest from the thirteenth century. A licensed inn in 1604, reputed to be the first in Scotland. Today the only remaining link in the chain of Moffat-Peebles coaching inns, it has had its share of praise and brickbats. "Cheery, clean little Crook Inn" and "one of the coldest-looking, cheerless places for travellers". The Crook's eccentricities were further emphasised when a Glasgow shipbuilder presented a reconstructed 1930s art decor "Crook Hotel" to his wife.

Tweedsmuir - The Crook Inn

Spacious and comfortable carpeted lounges and dining room, large enough for functions, lead to the eccentric bits. A pleasing staircase curves to the bedrooms with colour-coded tiled facilities. The ladies and gents loos, one up and one down, contain original art decor mirrors, tiles and plumbing (a quaint 1930s scale for the ladies). Adjacent to the gents is the Burns connection, "Willy Wastles Bar", built into the 1589 kitchen. Busy, welcoming, stone flagged with a historic central fireplace, its walls festooned with nick-nacks and its unusual chairs colourfully padded.

OPEN:	Hotel, 8am-12 midnight Bar, every day. 11am-12 midnight
TYPE:	Free House
ON DRAUGHT:	McEwan 80/-, Greenmantle Ale, McEwan's Tartan Special, Guinness, Carlsberg Lager, Taunton Cider
BOTTLED:	Traquair Bear Ale, Old Jock, Scottish Oatmeal Stout, Carlsberg Special Brew, selection of stout and cider
WHISKY:	Proprietary blends, plus 35/40 thought-provoking malts
WINE:	House white and red. A wine list of 44, with a few surprises for the connoisseur
FOOD:	Bar meals, 30 dishes plus a daily specials blackboard, during licensing hours. Lunch, high teas, dinner in the dining room. Afternoon teas in the lounge

ACCOMMODATION: 7 bedrooms, all with en-suite facilities
FACILITIES: Beer garden, children's play area, 7 miles of Tweed, plus loch fishing. Glass blowing in the stable of Upper Tweed Heritage Centre. Residents' drying room
OPEN FIRES: In the lounge, the bar has a realistic flame gas fire
WALKERS: Most welcome, as are fell racers, cyclists, fishers, etc.
CHILDREN: Welcome
DOGS: Not in the eating areas
PARKING: Car park, walkers' cars and route left by arrangement

FOOD

Variety and quality is the aim for the home-produced dishes. Steak and Greenmantle ale pie and the special grill are great favourites, as are the high teas, whilst vegetarians and children are certainly not forgotten.

ITEMS OF LOCAL INTEREST

The Crook was a Covenanter's refuge in the mid 1600s, one fugitive being hidden by a sympathetic landlady, "Jeanie o' the Crook", in the inn's stack of peats. A condemned Jacobite from the Crook escaped from his guards in '45 by shrouding himself in his plaid and tumbling

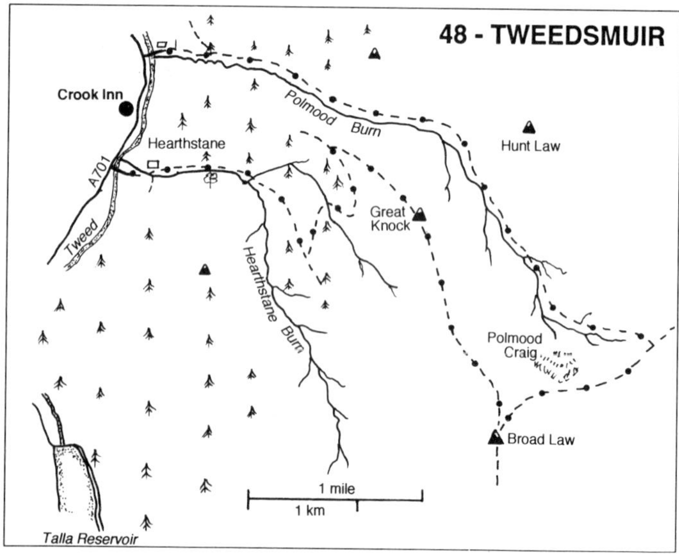

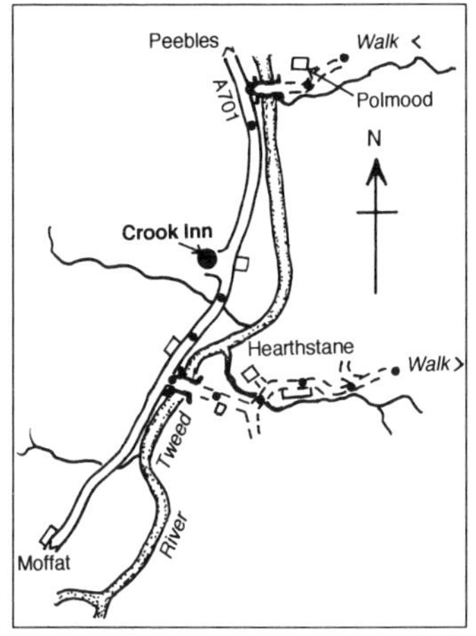

"hedgehog-like" into the black depths of the nearby Devil's Beef Tub. The literati also favoured The Crook: Robert Burns penned *Willy Wastles Wife* in the kitchen, Walter Scott enjoyed the hospitality, and John Buchan set many of his stirring tales in the area. In 1891 the Crook hosted the inaugural meet of The Scottish Mountaineering Club, prior to their ascent of Broad Law.

WALKS

The ascent of Broad Law, 10$^1/_2$ miles (16.8km) ascending 2018ft (615m). From The Crook walk S, turning left over the Tweed to Hearthstane. Continue E and S above Hearthstone Burn. At marker post No.55 on the forest road swing N, zig-zagging to Glenheurie Burn below the dome of Great Knock, 2267ft (691m). $^1/_2$ mile (0.8km) N of the burn crossing a gate leads right onto the shapely heathery ridge for 2 exhilarating miles (3.2km) SE to the grassy summit of Broad Law, 2756ft (840m). Ignore the CAA's metallic mushroom/tower and enjoy the endless rolling border hills. Descend E of the tower, with the fence, to the col below, swing left descending NW by Polmood Burn below the rock of Polmood Craig. 4 miles (6.4km) NW on fell and farm tracks, wind with the burn before entering the conifers and rounding the rear of Polmood to the Tweed and left to The Crook.

MOFFAT

49. BLACK BULL HOTEL - 1 Churchgate, Moffat, Dumfriesshire DG10 9EG. (01683) 20206 Fax (01683) 20483 ***Colour photo opposite p128***
Moffat lies in picturesque Annandale; 17 miles (27.2km) north of Lockerbie and 15$^1/_2$ miles (24.8km) south-west of St Mary's Loch, on the A701 and A708, close by the A74(T) and the Glasgow-Carlisle railway. The Black Bull is in the elbow of the A701 and A708.

SITUATION *OS Map Landranger. Sheet 78 1:50,000 GR 085051*
Records date back to 1568, though no doubt this white-walled inn succoured

travellers before that date. Today the old stables house horses of a different breed; the iron horse now occupies the Railway Bar and the cobbles ring to the clink of glasses and walkers' boots. This long bar is a "Births and Deaths" column for the age of steam: "1894 the West Highland Line" was born, "1954 Passenger Services in Moffat Withdrawn". Below the bar counter is a "foot-rail" from a length of the Caledonian line, above, an impressive array of ale dispensing devices and rows of shining bottles; it's not a quiet place, this bustling bar.

The Burn's Room lounge bar is a different affair, set in the original streetside inn with a soft light filtering through the bottle bottom glass; the gentle atmosphere insists walkers' boots are removed. A place to eat and drink in the cosy light and savour the words of Burns.

OPEN:	Sunday to Wednesday, 11am-11pm Thursday to Saturday, 11am-1am
TYPE:	Free House
ON DRAUGHT:	Guest ales on the blackboard, Wm McEwan 80/-, McEwan's 70/, Theakston B B, Younger's Tartan Special, McEwan's P A, Gillespies Malt Stout, Murphy's Irish Stout, Carlsberg Export Lager, Tennent's Lager, Dry Blackthorn Cider
BOTTLED:	Cherry, peach and apple flavoured beer. Plus a selection of beers, stout, lager and cider
WHISKY:	Proprietary blends, 30 to 40 selected malts, Irish and Rye
WINE:	House white, dry/medium/sweet; red. Thoughtful wine list
FOOD:	Bar, lounge bar and dining room, lunch 11.30am-2.15pm, supper 6.30-9.15pm; menu and specials blackboard
ACCOMMODATION:	7 double, 1 single, 6 en-suite 2 shared
FACILITIES:	Trestle tables in the open courtyard. Darts, dominoes, bandit, quiz machine, and "muzak" in the bar extension
OPEN FIRES:	In lounge bar
WALKERS:	Most welcome, no problems with tiled bar floor
CHILDREN:	Welcome in eating areas up to 9pm
DOGS:	OK
PARKING:	Off-street parking, plus market place

FOOD

Renowned for good value, home-cooked pub grub, made from local fresh produce and served with a smile. Specials such as cheese hot pot, the best of moist haggis and bread and butter pudding are popular with locals and energetic visitors.

ITEMS OF LOCAL INTEREST

The old Spa town, birthplace of Lord Dowding, is rich in legend and border fact. Moffat quartered Claverhouse's dragoons (the Covenanters' scourge) from 1682-85, Graham of Claverhouse lodging in the Black Bull. A pane of glass in the Burn's Room of the Black Bull bore Burn's scratchings of *To a Scrimpit Nature.* Epigram, glass, frame and all are reputed to languish in a Moscow museum. Burns also wrote the drinking song *O Willie Brew'd a Peck O' Malt* in the inn.

In 1831, the ill-fated coachman MacGeorge drove the Edinburgh mail into the snow-swept night; by Tweedshaws the coach foundered, MacGeorge shouting his last words into the wind, "Gang ye, bide ye, I gang on".

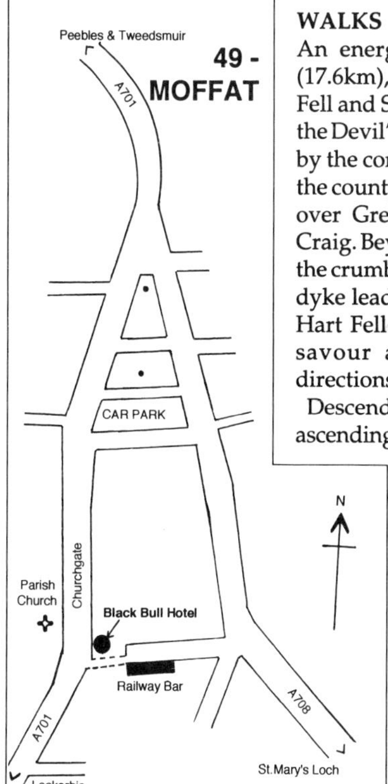

WALKS

An energetic linear walk of 11 miles (17.6km), ascending 1425ft (434m) to Hart Fell and Swatte Fell. 1/2 mile (0.8km) N of the Devil's Beef Tub, on the A701, turn NE by the conifers to Annanhead Hill where the county boundary guides the walker E over Great Hill, Chalk Rig and Spout Craig. Beyond Whitehope Heights follow the crumbling fence E and S to a sad stone dyke leading to the summit trig point of Hart Fell - a grandstand from which to savour an upland canvas from all directions.

Descend S and E with the fence before ascending Hartfell Craig to begin the finest valley rim walk in southern Scotland, SE via the edge of Swatte Fell and Blackhope Valley (care and experience essential) to descend steeply to Capplegill by the A708 in Moffat Water Valley.

A Walker's Guide to Moffat (50p) is available in the town.

Chapter 4
Outlyers

SEAHOUSES

50. THE OLDE SHIP HOTEL - Seahouses, Northumberland NE68 7RD. (01665) 720200. Fax (01665) 721383 ***Colour photo opposite p129***
The fishing port of Seahouses on the B1340, a section of the Scenic Coastal Route, is 22 miles (35.2km) south of Berwick-upon-Tweed and 14 miles (22.4km) north of Alnwick. The Olde Ship Hotel overlooks the harbour and the distant Farne Islands.

SITUATION *OS Map Landranger. Sheet 75 1:50,000 GR 220322*
A farmhouse in 1745, a licensed inn in 1812, this stone-built "ganzies and seaboots" local has been skippered by the present owner's family since 1910. The Ship is equally popular with those who "go down to the sea in ships" and those who secretly wished they had. For not only is it a manifestation of what a good pub should be, it is an atmospheric gem of seafaring mementos: creels and charts, lifeboat oars, sou'westers, blocks and binnacles, a mass of brass (polished every Sunday) sextants, anemometer, lamps, clocks and compasses. Friendly and swift service greet all who come aboard. Thank God they haven't got a parrot!

The panelled and planked saloon bar and split-level carpeted poop deck are furnished with iron tables, barrel stools, wall pews, stained glass windows and an open fire of glowing peats. Offering seasonal specialities it is an inviting bar and can become somewhat crowded at weekends, flooding into the hallway, the cabin bar, the family room and the harbour garden. Several Olde Ship lifebelts are at hand for over-indulgent customers. The dining room, lounge and boat gallery are tastefully decorated with nautical paintings, many by local artists.

OPEN:	Monday to Saturday, 11am-3pm, 6-11pm Sunday, 12 noon-3pm, 7-10.30pm
TYPE:	Free House
ON DRAUGHT:	Theakston XB & Best Bitter, Morland Speckled Hen, Longstone Bitter, Newcastle Exhibition & Bitter, McEwan's Best Scotch. Guinness, McEwan's Lager, Strong Bow Cider
BOTTLED:	Wee Heavy, Newcastle Brown Ale, Worthington White Shield, Carlsberg Special Brew, selection of stout, lager, cider

WHISKY:	Proprietary blends, plus a small selection of malts. Alnwick rum is popular
WINE:	House white, dry and medium; red. A thoughtful wine list
FOOD:	Lunches in the saloon and cabin bars, 12 noon-2.30pm. Dining room 12 noon-2.30pm. Afternoon tea in the lounge 3.30-5.30pm. Evening meals dining room only 7-8.30pm
ACCOMMODATION:	12 rooms all en-suite with additional facilities. 2 have four poster beds
FACILITIES:	Garden quoits pitch with seats. Electronic games in family room, dominoes in bar
OPEN FIRES:	Saloon bar, ornamental iron with marble surrounds
WALKERS:	Most welcome, the narrow entrance and bar doors ensure the removal of sacs
CHILDREN:	Welcome in the family room and dining room
DOGS:	No, only guide dogs
PARKING:	At the rear, walkers' cars left by arrangement

FOOD

Specials blackboards - front door, entrance hall and bar, plus menus. Generous sandwich/salad fillings, with crab a must. Home-cooked local specialities include crab soup, beef stovies, bosun's fish stew,

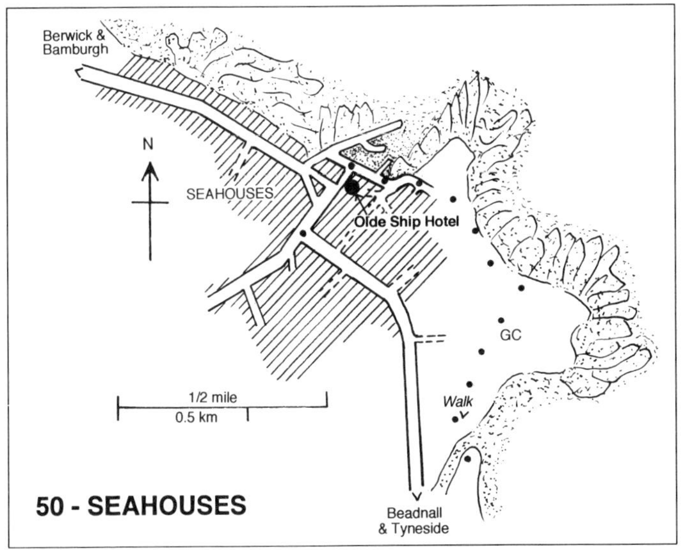

cheesy baked haddock and liver and onions: NO CHIPS. Clouty dumpling and tipsy log puds increase curiosity and waist lines.

ITEMS OF LOCAL INTEREST

Seahouses is at the centre of the golden beaches of Northumberland, with the castles of Alnwick, Warkworth, Dunstanburgh, Bamburgh and Lindisfarne within easy reach by foot or car. Bamburgh, birthplace of the heroine Grace Darling, overlooks the nature reserves of Budle Bay, Holy Island and the Farne Islands; boat trips for the Farnes leave regularly from Seahouses.

The humble kipper originated in Seahouses in 1843, John Woodger devised the "cold smoking" of herrings, naming the resultant delicacy "kipper".

WALKS

It would be unforgivable not to walk this magnificent coastline, 9 miles south to Craster. From Seahouses harbour walk S via the caravan park/ golf course onto the sands to Beadnell whose picturesque harbour heralds 2½ miles (4km) of beach and dune walking to the lichen-encrusted rocks of Newton Point (note the duck, including Eider) and Low Newton-by-the-Sea with its pub, The Ship. Continue S on the beach of Embleton Bay by the colourful chalets, to the fringes of Embleton golf course. A grassy path leads to the crumbling towers that were Dunstanburgh Castle - well worth a visit. 1¼ miles (2km) S past the rocks of Cushat Stiel, where cattle lick the salt pools and graze the seaweed, bring the walker to Craster's Kipper Smok'y and the Jolly Fisherman.

GIFFORD

51. GOBLIN HA' HOTEL - Main Street, Gifford, East Lothian EH41 4QH. (01620) 810244 Colour photo opposite p129

Nestling below the Lammermuir Hills, the village of Gifford surrounds the Y junction of B6355 and B6369; 20 miles (32km) south-east of Edinburgh and 4½ miles (7.2km) south of Haddington. The Goblin Ha' Hotel lines the main street and flanks the village square.

SITUATION *OS Map Landranger. Sheet 67 1:50,000 GR 533681*

Gifford village, popular with foot and motorised visitors, lies between the heathery Lammermuirs and the fertile plains of Lothian. A place of tranquil

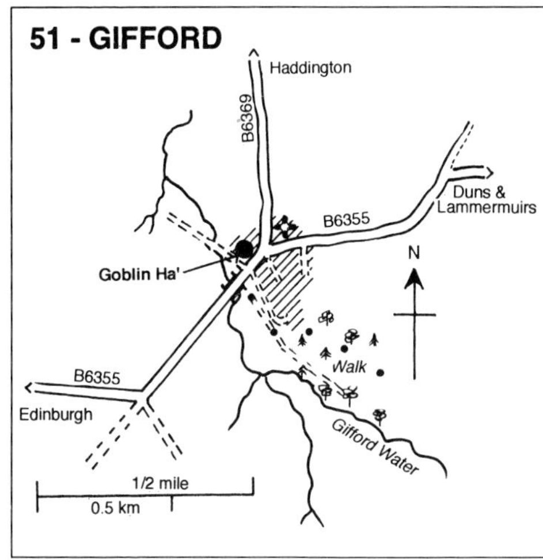

charm with its solid stone rows, village green, spires, towers and mercat cross. The white walls and painted margins of the friendly family-run Goblin Ha' Hotel make it instantly recognizable.

The self-contained public bar, dating from the 1750s, retains its authentic wood and stone ale-house atmosphere, with low wooden ceiling, fine open curved-back stone fireplace, long counter bedecked with hand pumps and shining taps dispensing well kept ales, wall settles and prints galore. A pool table and juke box are conveniently muffled in an adjacent room. In the late 1800s adjoining buildings were bought and the inn extended. The comfortable and stylish lounge bar with buttoned wall seats, pleasing prints and old maps is spacious, and the focal area for the hotel. Leading from it are the dining room, a delightful sun lounge, patio and garden pergola with picnic tables.

OPEN: Weekdays, 11am-2.30pm, 5-11pm
Saturday and Sunday, 11am-11pm

TYPE: Free House

ON DRAUGHT: Wm McEwan 80/-, Marston's Pedigree Bitter, Boddingtons Ale, Morland Speckled Hen, Young's Special, Theakston XB & BB, Younger's Special & PA, Guinness, Gillespie's Malt Stout, McEwan's Lager, Harp Lager, Blackthorn Dry Cider

BOTTLED: Theakston Bitter, Becks Bier, Grolsch, Carlsberg Special Brew, plus a selection of stout, lager and cider

WHISKY: Proprietary and de-luxe blends, single and blended malts

WINE: 5 house wines: white, dry/medium; red. Global wine list

FOOD: Bar and lounge bar, lunch 12.30-2pm, supper 6.30-9pm. Saturday and Sunday high tea, 5-6pm. Daily afternoon tea, 3-5pm

ACCOMMODATION: 2 double, 3 twin, 2 single, all en-suite

FACILITIES:	Sun lounge, patio/pergola with picnic tables, 2 acre gardens, boules court, pool table, darts, dominoes
OPEN FIRES:	Public bar and lounge bar
WALKERS:	Most welcome, pre-booked groups will be given washing/changing facilities if available, as will cyclists etc.
CHILDREN:	Welcome, children's licence
DOGS:	Allowed on a lead but not in the vicinity of food
PARKING	Streetside and in the square

FOOD

Prepared and cooked on the premises with seasonal vegetables grown in the Goblin Ha's garden; vegetarians and children well catered for. An innovative and hearty menu, with home-made casseroles, turkey/ham crepes. Mid-week steak suppers and Wednesday fondue very popular.

ITEMS OF LOCAL INTEREST

Before 1311, nearby Yester Castle was occupied by English troops. When recaptured by the Scots its keep was demolished, but the hall left intact. Later that century the site was levelled, above the Ha' of Sir Hugh Gifford, to form founds for the next castle. Thus the Ha' came to be buried yet still survived - the work of the Devil or possibly local Goblins? And so the name Goblin Ha' was spawned, mentioned in *Marmion* by Sir Walter Scott:

The same, whom ancient records call
The founder of the Goblin Hall.

WALKS

1) A woodland walk of 4 miles (6.4km) to the waters of Gifford and Hope. From the Goblin Ha' SSE with an avenue of beech to the lodge gates of Yester House, 25yds past on the left, by a Scots pine, a path leads E into the trees to join a woodland track E. This wood is a sylvan delight and as it thins take the path through a finger of trees running parallel to the track and as it rejoins the track, prior to Sunnyside, cross into the field. Walk S, by the fence, to Castle Wood below (the way by the fence is none too clear, but it is reputed to be a right of way). Rejoin a forest track descending to Gifford Water, swing left (E) to follow the distinct pathway by the water's edge joining Hope Water. Several small bridges are crossed as the way winds through this carpeted glen. At the wood's end turn and return by the outward route.

2) A 2 mile (3.2km) attempt to discover Yester Castle. Below Danskine Loch, GR 564673, a pathway leads SW with the burn into Castle Wood.

In the wood walk W with the water side track for $^{1}/_{2}$ mile (0.8km) to GR 552671 prior to a small bridge. A thin path ascends left (S) with the trees, fringing the new golf course, for $^{1}/_{4}$ mile (400m) to the barely visible castle remains (most difficult to find). Return by the outward path.

LEADBURN

52. LEADBURN INN - Leadburn, West Linton, Peeblesshire EH46 7BE. (01968) 672952

On the junction of A701, A702 and A720; 13 miles (20.8km) south of Edinburgh and $10^{1}/_{2}$ miles (16.8km) north of Peebles. The Leadburn Inn stands wedged in the northern fork of the village crossroads.

SITUATION *OS Map Landranger. Sheet 73 1:50,000 GR 234555*

Leadburn fringes a blasted moss and moorland that shivers between the Pentlands and the billows of the Moorfoots. Leadburn Inn, an ale-house and drover's rest, traces its history to 1777, when the Thomsons were licenced for "the Privilege and Liberty of Brewing, Baking, Vending and Retailing Ales". Gone is the old four square stone inn, today's exterior a mix of haphazard extensions. Internally the mood changes, a brick-floored conservatory, solidly furnished fronts the inn, leading to the bar

Leadburn - Leadburn Inn

and the lounge. The friendly bar is reminiscent of one in Glen Coe: stone floor, picture window, mirrors, wood tables, high-backed pews, coat stand, central pot-bellied stoves, and an upright piano. The lounge, warm and comfortable, L-shaped and carpeted, is suggestive of another age, its walls heavy with rural prints in gilded frames, racks of fusty books, china pots and potties. Well appointed bedrooms are up the stair, with the dining car lined up outside.

OPEN:	Every day, 11am-12 midnight
TYPE:	Free House
ON DRAUGHT:	One guest Ale, Caledonian 80/-, Tetley Bitter, Alloa Special, Alloa Export, Guinness, Carlsberg Lager, Castlemain XXXX, Addlestone's Cider, Strongbow Cider
BOTTLED:	Fowler's Wee Heavy, Newcastle Brown, Carlsberg Special Brew, plus a selection of beers, stout, lager and cider
WHISKY:	Proprietary blends and 15 selected malts
WINE:	House white, dry, medium and sweet; red burgundy. A thoughtful wine list of 35
FOOD:	Bar, lounge and conservatory, 12 noon-10pm. Breakfast 10am-12 noon. Carriage restaurant - dinner 6-10pm. Menus and gilt framed blackboards listing daily specials
ACCOMMODATION:	1 double 3 twin en-suite. 1 twin 1 single - shared facility
FACILITIES:	Darts, dominoes, cards, bandit, quiz nights, tabled patio
OPEN FIRES:	2 wood-burning pot-bellied stoves in the bar
WALKERS:	Welcome, "clatchie" boots restricted to the stones of the bar or the bricks of the conservatory
CHILDREN:	Welcome
DOGS:	In the bar
PARKING:	A sizeable car park; walkers' cars left by arrangement

FOOD

Leadburn Inn endeavours to provide a full range of home-cooked dishes including vegetarian, using local produce, throughout the day. A hefty Scottish breakfast, a light mid-day snack of chef's soup or shunter's stovies; for the later meal fresh trout or Border game pie.

ITEMS OF LOCAL INTEREST

In spite of John Buchan describing Leadburn as "The most villainous, bleak place I have ever seen" it is of interest. For the inn has worn many hats: a drover's rest, a coaching inn and a railway hotel. The inn was also a breakfast stop for the cyclists of the Waverley Road Club, who raced

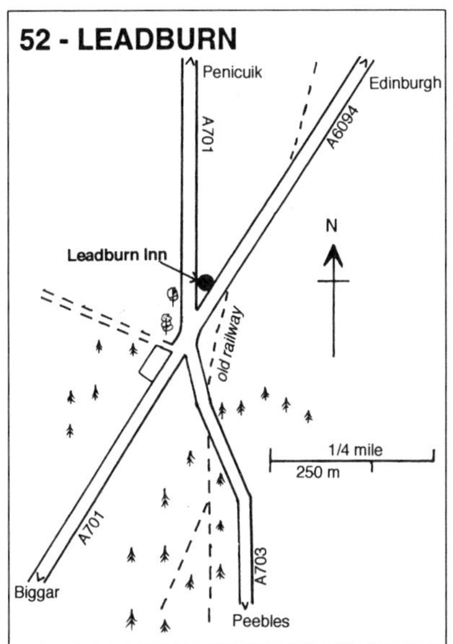

from Leadburn to Romano Bridge, on condition they washed in cold water from the outside tap before eating their bacon and eggs!

WALKS

Eddlestone Water leads S from the Leadburn Inn into the foothills of the Moorfoots, providing many fine and stimulating walks. The Dundreich and Blackhope Scar Horseshoe covers 10½ miles (16.8km) ascending 1778ft (542m) over four Donalds and their connecting ridges. From Gladhouse reservoir via Moorfoot farm ascend the NE shoulder of Jeffries Corse to Dundreich for a feast of views. With a boundary fence as guide, trek through heather and peat as the cirque horseshoes over Bowbeat, Emly Bank and Blackhope Scar before descending via The Kipps to the ruins of Hirendean Castle and Gladhouse.

NEWBIGGING

53. NESTLERS HOTEL - Dunsyre Road, Newbigging, Lanark ML11 8NA. (01555) 840680

On the north side of the A721, in the small isolated village of Newbigging, stands the cosy haven known as Nestlers Hotel; 2½ miles (4km) east of Carnwath and 20 miles (32km) west of Peebles. A Border approach route that wets the walker's appetite.

SITUATION *OS Map Landranger. Sheet 72 1:50,000 GR 014458*

Nestlers, born June 1988. Externally, something of an enigma, standing alongside the hollow eyed shells of the weaver's past. Internally, the welcoming blast of good cheer immediately blows away any doubts about entry; that is, if you make it past the Tongan coat of arms, the wooden green rooks and the old butter churn. One room doubles up as bar and social centre; a maverick of a pub it may be, but already a friendly chatty atmosphere exists in this isolated haven on these wild moors.

A roadside porch leads directly into the carpeted bar with its canopied counter, profusion of greenery and fine ceiling fan. Bare stone and wood panels surround the wall seats, tables and stools, and support the horns of stag and ox, in this room that is impossible to categorise. A small pleasant dining room leads off the bar, where meals can be enjoyed amidst a profusion of wood, bird boxes, shuttered windows and a fiddle. Even if you are not hungry try a bowl of soup!

OPEN:	11am-11.30pm, 1am if eating
TYPE:	Free House
ON DRAUGHT:	Dryboroughs 80/-, Skol Lager
BOTTLED:	Comprehensive selection of beer, stout, lager and cider
WHISKY:	Proprietary blends and a range of regional malts
WINE:	House, white - dry/medium/sweet; red. Interesting wine list of New World wines
FOOD:	Breakfast, lunch and supper 8am-9.30pm; in the bar or dining room (no smoking). Specials blackboard and menu
ACCOMMODATION:	3 twin en-suite
FACILITIES:	Darts, dominoes, chess, cards, trivial pursuits and quiz nights. Subdued background music
OPEN FIRES:	Lounge in winter
WALKERS:	Most welcome, please leave the countryside in the porch
CHILDREN:	Welcome if eating
DOGS:	Yes
PARKING:	Car park side and front

FOOD

Home cooking using fresh local produce, plus friendly helpful service. Specials such as beef steak pie, home-cooked ham in Pentland honey and cloves, bread and butter pudding and local cheese tempt and satisfy.

ITEMS OF LOCAL INTEREST

The once thriving weaver's village of thatched cottages and 500 souls has sadly dwindled to little more than one row of cottages and Nestlers; previously a post office, general store and agricultural engineers.

The Mercat Cross, standing by Dunsyre Road, was originally bound for the adjacent village of Elsrickle, however a heavy snow storm prevented its delivery and it was left at Newbigging for later collection.

The good folk of Elsrickle on returning for their Cross found it upright on its present site; and so it remains today.

Everything is nearby: Carstairs Junction for rail buffs, prehistoric settlements, Roman forts and Covenanter's Grave for walking historians.

Nestlers is a Tourist Information Point (TIP).

WALKS

8 mile (12.8km) walk, ascending 181ft (594m), to the Covenanter's Grave on Black Law. Park at Dunsyre walking E on the country lane to just beyond West Water; turn left onto the path running NW and N with the burn to Cairn Knowe and Black Law. The Grave of the Covenanter was requested by the occupant to enable him to see his beloved Ayrshire hills. Return S to Cairn Knowe then W over the bealach of The Pike and Bleak Law. Continuing W to Left Law, then S on Stonypath and then E past the school, by road to Dunsyre.

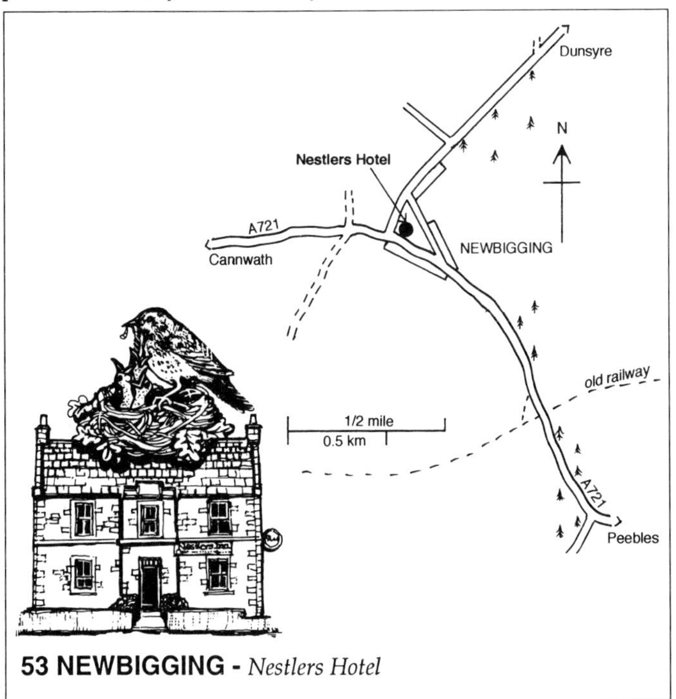

53 NEWBIGGING - *Nestlers Hotel*

GLOSSARY

Lowland Scots (Sc) Northumbrian (N)

Ba' (Sc)	Ball of leather stuffed with wet moss/paper, used in Border games
Bide (Sc)	Stay
Bit (Sc)	Little, small
Black Lead	Leaded polish used to clean and blacken iron fires/ovens
Brig (Sc)	Bridge
Ca-ed (Sc)	Called
Canny (N)	Good, fine; a reluctant/begrudging grand or great
Clatchie (Sc)	Mud or mire covered
Clarts/clarty(N)	as Clatchie
Clippie mat (N)	Hand-woven mats, using remnants of household material
Clouty dumpling/cloutie(Sc,N)	A dried fruit confection steamed slowly in a cloth or 'clout'. A superb pudding, but heavy
Crack (N)	Talk, animated and friendly
Cromlech (Sc)	Dolmen, two large upright stones supporting a large flat stone
Dar'say (N)	Dare say, know
Deid (Sc)	Dead
Doonies (Sc)	Married men or outsiders, a team in Hand Ba' game
Dour (Sc)	Severe, serious
Driech (Sc)	Long, tiresome, as in a wet day
Drouthy (Sc)	Dry, thirsty
Fasten E'en/Fasten's Eve(Sc)	Shrove Tuesday in Denholm
Fettle (Sc,N)	Feeling, mood
Fiere (Sc)	Partner
Fra quhilk(Sc)	From which
Gae (Sc)	Very
Gang (Sc,N)	Go, depart
Ganzie (N)	Seaman's heavy woollen sweater, Northumbrian derivative of Guernsey sweater
Gedholes (Sc)	Pools
Gin-gang (N)	Animal shelter in farmyard
Gizened (Sc)	Dried up, withered
Guid willie waught (Sc)	Friendly draught
Haugh (Sc,N)	Flat fertile riverside land
Hemmel (N)	Cattle/stock yard or shelter
Hoolit/howlet(Sc)	Young owl
Howff (Sc)	Ale-house, inn, pub
Hoy/hoyed (N)	Throw/thrown
Ilk (Sc)	The same, a name the same as an ancestral estate
Ken (Sc)	Know

Kine/kye (Sc)	Cows/cattle
Leuk (Sc)	Look
Lonnen (N)	Farm or cart track
Loup (Sc,N)	Leap, jump
Mercat (Sc)	Market
Neuk (N)	Nook, corner
Nolte (N)	Cattle
Pele (Sc,N)	Tower, defensive stronghold
Quoiting haugh	Flat field at riverside for game of quoits
Raptores (N)	Birds of prey with hooked bills and sharp claws
Reek (Sc)	Smoke or vapour
Reiver (Sc,N)	Robber/raider or partisan/freedom fighter
Retted (Sc)	Softening of flax fibres
Snicket (N)	Narrow lined path or gate
Stotties (N)	Flat buns from bread dough, in which the yeast had ceased working. Cooked in a "hot bottomed oven"
Stovies (Sc)	Potatoes, onions and left over scraps of beef; cooked slowly in beef dripping
Tackity boots(Sc,N)	Shepherd's waterproof boots with studded curved soles
Uppies (Sc)	single men/town or village men, a team in Hand Ba' game
Wab (Sc)	Web
Wabster (Sc)	Flax/linen weavers

RECOMMENDED READING

Brave Borderland, H.Drummond Gauld (Thomas Nelson & Sons Ltd, Edinburgh)

Highways & Byeways, Andrew and John Lang (Macmillan and Co Ltd, London)

Journey through Britain, John Hillaby (World Books, London)

Refreshing the Spirit in Jedburgh, Garrett O'Brien (The Crochet Factory, Jedburgh)

The Borders, F.R.Banks (B.T.Batsford Ltd, London)

The Border Country - A Walker's Guide, Alan Hall (Cicerone Press, Milnthorpe)

The Steel Bonnets, George MacDonald Fraser (Pan Books, London)

The Story of ELSDON, G.N.Taylor (St Cuthbert's Church, Elsdon)

This Unknown Island, S.P.B.Mais (Bodley Head, London)

Tibbie Shiels, R.George Ballantyne (The Southern Annual)

Plus the many interesting publications relating specifically to Border towns and surrounding districts available at local bookshops and Tourist Information Centres. Not forgetting the CAMRA newsletter, FOC at the majority of Border pubs/inns.

ALPHABETICAL INDEX OF PUBS/INNS

PRINTED BY
CARNMOR PRINT & DESIGN, LONDON RD, PRESTON